W9-CBL-165

# MLA Handbook for Writers of Research Papers

Second Edition

Joseph Gibaldi
Walter S. Achtert

The Modern Language Association of America
New York                                    1984

Copyright © 1977, 1984 by The Modern Language Association of America

**Library of Congress Cataloging in Publication Data**

Modern Language Association of America.
  MLA handbook for writers of research papers.

  Rev. ed. of: MLA handbook for writers of research
papers, theses, and dissertations. 1st ed. 1977.
  Includes index.
  1. English language—Rhetoric—Handbooks, manuals, etc.
2. Report writing—Handbooks, manuals, etc.   3. Bibliography—Methodology—Handbooks, manuals, etc.   4. Bibliographical citations—Handbooks, manuals, etc.   I. Gibaldi,
Joseph, 1942-    .   II. Achtert, Walter S.   III. Modern
Language Association of America. MLA handbook for
writers of research papers, theses, and dissertations.
IV. Title.   V. Title: M.L.A. handbook for writers of
research papers.
PE1478.M57   1984        808'.02        84-10819
ISBN 0-87352-132-3

Cover design by Michael Soha.

Published by The Modern Language Association of America
62 Fifth Avenue, New York, New York 10011
First printing

# MLA Handbook for Writers of Research Papers

Second Edition

# CONTENTS

# Contents

# PREFACE FOR THE INSTRUCTOR

For more than four decades, the style recommended by the MLA for scholarly manuscripts and student research papers has been widely adopted not only by journals and university presses but also by graduate schools, college departments, and individual instructors. Based on *The MLA Style Sheet* (1951; rev. 1970), which was compiled for literary and linguistic scholars who publish in learned journals, the first edition of the *MLA Handbook* was published in 1977 to meet the pedagogical need for a book that would incorporate the MLA style guidelines and serve as a supplementary text in a writing course or as a reference book for undergraduates to use independently. The extraordinary publication success of the *Handbook* throughout the United States, Canada, and other countries (a Japanese translation appeared in 1980) testifies to the continuing need, by both instructors and students, for such a teaching and research tool.

The recent revisions in MLA style, after years of study and deliberation by various MLA committees as well as by the association's Executive Council, compelled a second edition of the *Handbook*. The most important change is the adoption of a new system of documentation: brief parenthetical citations in the text refer to a bibliography at the end of the research paper and thus eliminate the need for all but explanatory footnotes or endnotes. The other mechanical changes involved are also intended to make scholarly documentation simpler, more consistent, and more efficient. (For the convenience of instructors who prefer a different system, this edition continues to provide guidance on using notes and to describe alternative methods.)

The new edition has given us the opportunity to incorporate suggestions received from instructors during the past seven years. In addition, the simultaneous publication of a companion volume, *The MLA Style Manual*, a comprehensive style guide for scholars and graduate students, has allowed us to focus this edition of the *Handbook* more sharply on its primary audience: the undergraduate student. We have tried to clarify any ambiguities, to amplify matters only touched on previously, and to offer additional, and updated, examples when needed. This edition also expands the section on documenting nonprint sources (e.g., films, television programs, recordings, computer software, information from a computer service). To assist the student in spacing and indentation, examples have once again been reproduced in typescript, rather than set in type.

For the instructor who wishes to use the *MLA Handbook* as a class text, chapter 1 provides an expanded discussion of the general question of research and writing: approaching the research paper, selecting a topic, using the library, compiling a working bibliography, taking notes, avoiding plagiarism, preparing an outline, and writing the paper. This edition, like its predecessor, offers chapters on the mechanics of writing (spelling, punctuation, names of persons, numbers, titles in the text, and quotations), on the format of the research paper (typing, paper, margins, spacing, etc.), and on abbreviations and reference words. The chapters "Preparing the List of Works Cited" and "Documenting Sources" contain detailed instructions on using the MLA documentation style.

Aimed specifically at writers of research papers, the *MLA Handbook* pays only minimal attention to the problems that these writers share with all other writers. Questions of usage and writing style have been left, for the most part, to the many excellent manuals in that field.

Although it would be impossible to acknowledge everyone who assisted us with this project, we would like to express our gratitude to a number of persons who read and commented on several drafts of the *Handbook* and who offered us valuable advice and practical suggestions at various stages of its preparation: John Algeo, Richard Bjornson, Eric J. Carpenter, Thomas Clayton, Robert A. Colby, Richard H. Cracroft, Robert J. Di Pietro, Richard J. Dunn, Bertie E. Fearing, John H. Fisher, John C. Gerber, Barbara Q. Gray, Martin Green, Stephen Greenblatt, Laurel T. Hatvary, Carolyn G. Heilbrun, Weldon A. Kefauver, Gwin J. Kolb, Richard A. LaFleur, Sarah N. Lawall, William T. Lenehan, Richard Lloyd-Jones, William D. Lutz, Sylvia Kasey Marks, Margaret McKenzie, Harrison T. Meserole, George J. Metcalf, Susan P. Miller, James V. Mirollo, William G. Moulton, Judith S. Neaman, John Neubauer, Stephen M. North, Mary Ann O'Donnell, Margaret C. Patterson, Nancy S. Rabinowitz, James L. Rolleston, Barbara Rotundo, Jeffrey L. Sammons, Carole G. Silver, David Staines, William R. Streitberger, Madeleine B. Therrien, Vincent L. Tollers, Mario J. Valdés, Renée Waldinger, Jerry W. Ward, Day Werking, Jr., Katharina M. Wilson, Linda L. Wyman, and Robert F. Yeager.

We would also like to give special thanks to Judith H. Altreuter, R. Neil Beshers, Claire Cook, Judy Goulding, Elizabeth Holland, Barbara S. LaBarba, Bonnie Levy, Hans Rütimann, Roslyn Schloss, English Showalter, Elaine S. Silver, and all our other colleagues on the MLA staff for their unfailing support and help.

# PREFACE FOR THE STUDENT

The *MLA Handbook for Writers of Research Papers* describes a set of conventions governing the written presentation of research. The recommendations on the mechanics and format of the research paper reflect the practices recommended by the Modern Language Association of America (a professional organization of more than 25,000 instructors of English and other languages) and required by college teachers throughout the United States and Canada. Questions of writing style—choice of words, sentence structure, tone, and so on—are covered in other guides, such as those listed in section 1.9, and are not considered here.

Chapter 1 discusses the logical steps in research and writing—selecting a topic, using the library, compiling a working bibliography, taking notes, avoiding plagiarism, preparing an outline, and writing. Chapter 2 concerns the mechanics of writing (e.g., punctuation, spelling, capitalization, and the treatment of quotations and titles in the text), and chapter 3 deals with the formal preparation of the manuscript—typing and binding the paper. Chapter 4, on preparing the list of works cited, provides well over two hundred examples illustrating bibliographic forms for both printed and other sources often referred to in research papers (e.g., films, recordings, and computer materials), and chapter 5 explains how to document such sources in the text. Following chapter 6, on abbreviations and reference words, the book concludes with sample pages from a research paper and a subject index.

The *MLA Handbook* is intended as both a classroom text and a reference tool. If you read it through first from cover to cover, you may find it easier to use later when you consult it for specific recommendations. The chapters are divided into numbered sections and subsections, and by citing these, rather than page numbers, the index makes it easy to find the information you need.

# 1 RESEARCH AND WRITING

## 1.1. The research paper

Whether you are writing your first or your fifteenth research paper, it is important to remember that a research paper is, first and foremost, a form of written communication. Yet when assigned a research paper, many students become so preoccupied with gathering material, taking notes, compiling a bibliography, and documenting sources that they forget to apply the knowledge and skills they have acquired through previous writing experiences. This discussion, therefore, begins with a brief review of the steps often outlined for writing. Although few writers follow such formal steps, keeping them in mind can suggest ways to proceed as you write.

1. If given a choice, select a subject that interests you and that you can treat within the assigned limits of time and space.

2. Determine your purpose in writing the paper. (For example, do you want to describe something, explain something, argue for a certain point of view, or persuade your reader to think or do something?)

3. Write a thesis statement expressing the central idea of your paper.

4. Consider the type of audience you are writing for. (For example, is your reader a specialist or a nonspecialist on the subject, someone likely to agree or disagree with you, someone likely to be interested or uninterested in the subject?)

5. Gather your ideas and information in a preliminary list, eliminating anything that would weaken your paper.

6. Arrange materials in an order appropriate to the aims of the paper and decide on the method or methods you will use in developing your ideas (e.g., definition, classification, analysis, comparison and contrast, example).

7. Make a detailed outline to help you keep to your plan as you write.

8. Write a preliminary draft, making sure that you have a clearcut introduction, body, and conclusion.

9. Read your preliminary draft critically and try to improve it, rewording, rearranging, adding, and eliminating phrases to make the writing more effective. Follow the same procedure with each subsequent draft.

10. Proofread the final draft, making all final corrections.

As you prepare and write research papers, always remember that no set of conventions for preparing a manuscript can replace lively and intelligent writing and that no amount of research and documentation can compensate for poor writing.

Although the research paper has much in common with other forms of writing, it differs from them in relying on sources of information other than the writer's personal knowledge and experience. It is based on either primary research, the study of a subject through firsthand observation and investigation, or secondary research, the examination of studies that others have made of the subject. Many academic papers, as well as many reports and proposals required in business, government, and the professions, depend on secondary research.

Research into a topic will enlarge your knowledge and understanding of a subject and will often lend authority to your ideas and opinions. The paper based on research is not a collection of others' thoughts but a carefully constructed presentation of an idea—or a number of ideas— that relies on other sources for clarification and verification. Facts and opinions drawn from outside sources must be fully documented, usually through parenthetical references in the text to sources listed at the end of the paper. The documentation, however, should do no more than support your statements and provide concise information about the research cited; it should never overshadow the paper or distract the reader from the ideas you present.

## 1.2. Selecting a topic

All writing begins with a topic. If you have some freedom in choosing what to write about, look for a subject that interests you and that will maintain your interest throughout the various stages of research and writing. Some preliminary reading in the library will help you determine the extent of your interest. A library visit can also reveal whether enough serious work has been done on the subject to permit adequate research and whether the pertinent source materials are readily available.

In selecting a topic, keep in mind the time allotted to you and the expected length of the research paper. "Twentieth-Century Literature" would obviously not be a suitable choice for a ten-page term paper. Students commonly begin with fairly general topics and then refine them, by research and thought, into more specific ones. Here again, preliminary reading will be helpful. Consult books and articles as well as some general reference works, such as encyclopedias, and try to narrow your topic by focusing on a particular aspect or a particular approach. The student whose initial topic is "The Imagery of Wordsworth's *Prelude*," for instance, might decide, after some careful thought and reading, to write on "Nature Imagery in Book 1 of Wordsworth's *Prelude*"; the topic "Modern Aviation" could likewise be narrowed to "The Future of the Space Shuttle."

Before beginning the project, make sure you understand the amount and depth of research required, the degree of subjectivity permitted, and the type of paper expected. Confer with your instructor if you need help in understanding the assignment or in choosing an appropriate topic.

## 1.3. Using the library

Since most of your research papers will make use of the works of experts and scholars, you should become thoroughly acquainted with the libraries to which you have access. Many academic libraries offer programs of orientation and instruction to meet the needs of all students, the freshman as well as the graduate student. There may be pamphlets or handbooks introducing researchers to the library, guided tours, and lectures or even courses on using the library.

Nearly all public and academic libraries have desks staffed by professional reference librarians who can help you locate information and inform you of the instructional programs offered by the library. For a comprehensive introduction to the library, consult such books as Jean Key Gates, *Guide to the Use of Libraries and Information Sources* (5th ed., New York: McGraw, 1983), and Margaret G. Cook, *New Library Key* (3rd ed., New York: Wilson, 1975). Useful for reference works in literary studies are Margaret C. Patterson, *Literary Research Guide* (2nd ed., New York: MLA, 1983), and Nancy L. Baker, *A Research Guide for Undergraduate Students: English and American Literature* (New York: MLA, 1982).

The first step in getting to know your library is learning to use the central card catalog or, if the files are stored in a computer, the on-line catalog. Books are usually listed in the catalog by author, title, and subject. In some libraries, author cards, title cards, and subject cards are arranged alphabetically in a single catalog. Most libraries, however, divide the cards into two catalogs (author and title cards in one, subject cards in the other) or, more rarely, into three catalogs (one each for authors, titles, and subjects).

Next, become familiar with the two systems of classification most frequently used in American libraries: the Dewey Decimal system and the Library of Congress system. The Dewey Decimal system classifies books under ten major headings:

| | |
|---|---|
| 000 | General works |
| 100 | Philosophy |

| 200 | Religion |
| 300 | Social sciences |
| 400 | Language |
| 500 | Natural sciences |
| 600 | Technology and applied sciences |
| 700 | Fine arts |
| 800 | Literature |
| 900 | History and geography |

The Library of Congress system divides books into twenty major groups:

| A | General works |
| B | Philosophy and religion |
| C | General history |
| D | Foreign history |
| E-F | American history |
| G | Geography and anthropology |
| H | Social sciences |
| J | Political science |
| K | Law |
| L | Education |
| M | Music |
| N | Fine arts |
| P | Language and literature |
| Q | Science |
| R | Medicine |
| S | Agriculture |
| T | Technology |
| U | Military science |
| V | Naval science |
| Z | Bibliography and library science |

If you know the author of a book, you can locate it by consulting the author card. The combination of letters and numbers in the upper left-hand corner of the card (PS3521 .A7255 Z462) is the designation by which the book is shelved in the library. The top few lines of the card contain the author's name and date of birth (Kauffmann, Stanley, 1916–), the full title of the book (*Albums of Early Life*), and complete publication information (published by Ticknor & Fields in the city of New Haven in the year 1980). The next few lines, in smaller print, describe the physical characteristics of the book (229 pages of text, 22 cm. in height) and give the International Standard Book Number (0-89919-015-4). The lower half of the card shows the subject entries under which the book is also cataloged (Kauffmann, Stanley, 1916– —Biography; Authors, American—20th century—Biography; Critics—United States—Biography), the Library of Congress classification number (PS3521.A7255Z462), the Dewey Decimal number (818'.5203), the alternate Dewey classification (B, for biography), and the Library of Congress catalog card number (80-14481).

---

PS3521
.A7255
Z462    **Kauffmann, Stanley,** 1916-
       Albums of early life / Stanley Kauffmann. — New Haven :
Ticknor & Fields, 1980.

       229 p. ; 22 cm.
       ISBN 0-89919-015-4

       1. Kauffmann, Stanley, 1916-     —Biography.    2. Authors, American—
      20th century—Biography.    3. Critics—United States—Biography.    I. Title.

       PS3521.A7255Z462          818'.5203          80-14481
                               ₍B₎                 MARC

      Library of Congress

---

If you know only the title of a book, you can locate it by consulting the title card, which differs from the author card only in that the title of the book appears at the top of the card.

---

         **Albums of early life**
PS3521
.A7255
Z462    **Kauffmann, Stanley,** 1916-
       Albums of early life / Stanley Kauffmann. — New Haven :
Ticknor & Fields, 1980.

       229 p. ; 22 cm.
       ISBN 0-89919-015-4

       1. Kauffmann, Stanley, 1916-     —Biography.    2. Authors, American—
      20th century—Biography.    3. Critics—United States—Biography.    I. Title.

       PS3521.A7255Z462          818'.5203          80-14481
                               ₍B₎                 MARC

      Library of Congress

If you have no author or title in mind but wish to find a book or books on a particular topic, consult the subject card, which differs from the author card only in that the subject appears at the top of the card. (See *Library of Congress Subject Headings*, or the list your library follows, to find the appropriate headings.)

---

PS3521         Critics--United States--Biography
.A7255
Z462     **Kauffmann, Stanley,** 1916-
          Albums of early life / Stanley Kauffmann. — New Haven : Ticknor & Fields, 1980.
          229 p. ; 22 cm.
          ISBN 0-89919-015-4

          1. Kauffmann, Stanley, 1916-       —Biography.    2. Authors, American—20th century—Biography.    3. Critics—United States—Biography.    I. Title.
          PS3521.A7255Z462        818'.5203        80-14481
                                     [B]          MARC

Library of Congress

---

Besides knowing how to locate books on specific subjects, you should also know the range of general reference works available to you, such as dictionaries, encyclopedias, biographical works, yearbooks, atlases, and gazetteers. The following are among the most widely used:

## Dictionaries

*Webster's Third New International Dictionary of the English Language*
*Oxford English Dictionary*

## Encyclopedias

*Columbia Encyclopedia*
*Encyclopedia Americana*
*Encyclopaedia Britannica*
*Collier's Encyclopedia*

## Biographical works for persons no longer living

*Dictionary of American Biography* (for the United States)
*Dictionary of Canadian Biography*
*Dictionary of National Biography* (for Great Britain)
*Webster's Biographical Dictionary* (also includes persons still living)

## Biographical works for persons still living

*Contemporary Authors*
*Current Biography*

*International Who's Who*
*Webster's Biographical Dictionary* (also includes persons no longer
   living)
*Who's Who in America*

### Yearbooks
*Americana Annual*
*Britannica Book of the Year*
*Europa Year Book*

### Atlases
*Times Atlas of the World*
*National Atlas of the United States of America*

### Gazetteers
*Columbia-Lippincott Gazetteer of the World*
*Webster's New Geographical Dictionary*


You should know, too, that all major fields of study have specialized
dictionaries and encyclopedias, which are also useful sources for preliminary reading in a subject. The following are just a sampling:

### Art
*Encyclopedia of World Art*
*McGraw-Hill Dictionary of Art*
*Oxford Companion to Art*

### Astronomy
*Cambridge Encyclopaedia of Astronomy*
*Larousse Encyclopedia of Astronomy*

### Biology
*Dictionary of Biology*
*Encyclopedia of the Biological Sciences*

### Chemistry
*Condensed Chemical Dictionary*
*Encyclopedia of Chemistry*

### Computer science
*Computer Dictionary and Handbook*
*Encyclopedia of Computer Science*

### Dance
*Concise Oxford Dictionary of Ballet*
*Encyclopedia of Dance and Ballet*

### Earth sciences

*Cambridge Encyclopaedia of Earth Sciences*
*Encyclopedia of Earth Sciences*

### Economics

*Encyclopedia of Economics*
*McGraw-Hill Dictionary of Modern Economics*

### Education

*Encyclopedia of Education*

### Film

*Dictionary of Films*
*International Encyclopedia of Film*
*Oxford Companion to Film*

### History

*Dictionary of American History*
*Encyclopedia of World History*

### Law

*Black's Law Dictionary*
*Encyclopedic Dictionary of International Law*

### Literature

*Cassell's Encyclopaedia of World Literature*
*Oxford Companion to American Literature*
*Oxford Companion to Canadian Literature*
*Oxford Companion to Classical Literature*
*Oxford Companion to English Literature*
*Oxford Companion to French Literature*
*Oxford Companion to German Literature*
*Oxford Companion to Spanish Literature*
*Penguin Companion to American Literature*
*Penguin Companion to Classical, Oriental, and African Literature*
*Penguin Companion to English Literature*
*Penguin Companion to European Literature*

### Mathematics

*Prentice-Hall Encyclopedia of Mathematics*
*Universal Encyclopedia of Mathematics*

### Medicine

*Stein and Day International Medical Encyclopedia*
*Dorland's Medical Dictionary*

## Music

*Harvard Dictionary of Music*
*New Grove Dictionary of Music and Musicians*
*Oxford Companion to Music*

## Philosophy

*Dictionary of Philosophy*
*Encyclopedia of Philosophy*

## Physics

*Encyclopaedic Dictionary of Physics*
*Encyclopedia of Physics*

## Psychology

*Encyclopedia of Psychology*

## Religion

*Encyclopaedia of Religion and Ethics*
*International Standard Bible Encyclopedia*

## Science and technology

*Harper Encyclopedia of Science*
*McGraw-Hill Encyclopedia of Science and Technology*

## Social sciences

*Dictionary of Social Sciences*
*International Encyclopedia of the Social Sciences*

Articles in specialized reference works often provide brief bibliographies that can help in the early stages of research. To find additional, including more recent, material and information on a subject, you can turn to indexes, bibliographies, and abstracts. The *New York Times Index* offers a guide to news stories and feature articles in that newspaper. Indexes are also published for many other newspapers, including the *Chicago Tribune, Christian Science Monitor, Los Angeles Times, New Orleans Times-Picayune,* and *Washington Post.*

The widely known and much used *Readers' Guide to Periodical Literature,* which began publication in 1900, is an index to the contents of popular journals and magazines. (For periodical literature published before 1900 or in other countries, consult the appropriate sources in your library.) Also useful is the *Essay and General Literature Index,* which lists essays and articles published in books.

Just as the various subject areas have their own reference works, they also have specialized indexes, such as the following:

**Art**
*Art Index*

**Biology**
*Biological and Agricultural Index*

**Business**
*Business Periodicals Index*

**Chemistry**
*Current Abstracts of Chemistry and Index Chemicus*

**Classical studies**
*L'année philologique*

**Education**
*Education Index*

**Engineering**
*Engineering Index Monthly and Author Index*

**Humanities**
*British Humanities Index*
*Humanities Index*

**Language and literature**
*MLA International Bibliography*

**Law**
*Index to Legal Periodicals*

**Medicine**
*Index Medicus*

**Music**
*Music Index*

**Philosophy**
*Philosopher's Index*

**Religion**
*Religion Index One: Periodicals*

**Science and technology**
*Applied Science and Technology Index*
*General Science Index*
*Science Citation Index*

**Social sciences**
*Social Sciences Index*

Abstracting services provide useful summaries of the contents of journal articles. Among the many reference works of this type are the following:


*Abstracts in Anthropology*
*Biological Abstracts*
*Chemical Abstracts*
*Historical Abstracts*
*Key to Economic Science*
*Language and Language Behavior Abstracts*
*Physics Abstracts*
*Psychological Abstracts*
*Religious and Theological Abstracts*
*RILA* (art)
*RILM* (music)
*Science Abstracts*
*Sociological Abstracts*


Summaries of doctoral dissertations are available in *Dissertation Abstracts International* (entitled *Dissertation Abstracts* until 1969), which is divided into three series: "A" for the humanities and social sciences, "B" for the sciences, and "C" for European dissertations.

Library books are kept either on open shelves, to which the public has direct access, or in closed stacks. To obtain a book in closed stacks you usually have to present a call slip to a library staff member, who will locate the book for you. Regardless of the system used, all libraries keep some books separate from the main collection. If a book is kept in a special area, the catalog card should show the location. For example, in some libraries an "f" preceding the call number on the card means "folio size" and shows that the book is shelved with oversized books. The word "Reserved" on a card indicates a book is currently required in a course and stored in a special section, at the instructor's request, to keep it available for students in the course and, usually, to confine its use to the library. A book shelved in the reference section, designated by an "R" or "Ref." on the catalog card, may also be used only in the library. Some libraries have additional special collections, such as rare books or government documents, that are kept separate from the main collection.

Libraries also commonly set aside specific areas for various types of materials—current periodicals, pamphlets, clippings, and nonprint materials, such as pictures, maps, films, slides, recordings, videotapes, and audiotapes. Consult the library directory or the librarian for locations.

In addition to using these print and nonprint materials, the researcher should be familiar with microforms as well as with the resources provided by computer technology. "Microform" designates printed matter greatly reduced in size by microphotography; common types are the microfilm, microcard, and microfiche. Each microform may be magnified by the use of a special reader. Library staff members are usually on hand specifically to help you locate microform materials and use the readers.

Some academic libraries also provide computer terminals that have direct access to data bases. By communicating key words and names to the computer, you can obtain bibliographic references for your specific project. The list resulting from a computer search appears on the terminal's screen, but it may also be available in printout form. Some distributors of data-base services, such as the Educational Resources Information Center (ERIC), have both an information storage system and a retrieval system—that is, they supply not only bibliographic references but also copies of the documents themselves.

Although not all libraries provide computer assistance, most do offer researchers other services you should know about, such as copying facilities and interlibrary loans. If, for example, your library does not have the sources you need, ask whether it can borrow them from another library. If it can, consult the *National Union Catalog* to find out which libraries have the books you want or, if you need periodicals, the *Union List of Serials* and *New Serial Titles*. Some nearby libraries have mutual agreements that make the exchange of research materials as quick and inexpensive as possible.

Obviously, the more you know about the library and the materials and services it provides, the more successful you will be in gathering information and ideas for your research paper.

## 1.4. Compiling a working bibliography

The first stage in research is discovering where to look for information and opinions on your topic. Begin by compiling a "working bibliography"—a list of books, journal articles, and other sources to be consulted. Your preliminary reading in both general and specialized reference works will probably provide you with the first titles for this list. You can add others by consulting appropriate subject cards in the card catalog and checking indexes and bibliographies, such as those mentioned in the last section. During your research be sure to read carefully through the bibliography and notes of each book and article you read on your topic; more often than not, your reading will lead you to additional important sources. Your working bibliography will frequently change during your research as you add new titles and eliminate those that do not prove useful and as you explore and emphasize certain aspects of your subject rather than others. The working bibliography evolves into the "final bibliography," the list of works cited that appears at the end of the research paper.

Many instructors suggest that students use index cards in compiling the working bibliography—one card for each source. Index cards allow much greater flexibility than does a continuous list on sheets of paper. For example, as you research, you can arrange, and rearrange, your sources however you wish (e.g., in alphabetical order, in chronological order by date of publication, in order of relevance to your topic) and as often as you wish with little inconvenience; index cards also permit you to divide sources into different groups (e.g., those already consulted and those not yet consulted, those most useful and those less so).

In adding sources to your working bibliography, write down *all* the publication information needed for the final bibliography. For a book, record the author's full name, the full title (including any subtitle), the edition (if it is a second or later edition), the number of volumes, the city of publication (write down only the first if several cities are listed), the publisher, and the year of publication. For an article in a popular periodical, such as a newspaper or a magazine, include the author's name, the title of the article, the title of the periodical, the date of publication, and the inclusive page numbers of the article (i.e., the number of the page on which the article begins, a hyphen, and the number of the page on which the article ends). For an article in a scholarly journal, include the author's name, the title of the article, the title of the journal, the volume number, the year of publication, and the inclusive page numbers of the article. (See ch. 4 for complete information on compiling the final bibliography of the research paper.)

In addition, at the bottom of the index card note the exact source of the bibliographic information, in case you need to recheck the source or to borrow the material from another library (a library often requires a printed source for verification before it will accept a request for an interlibrary loan). Leave room, too, in the upper right-hand corner of the card, to record the call number or any other identifying information needed to locate the work.

> Porter, Dennis. *The Pursuit of Crime:*     PN
> *Art and Ideology in Detective*     3448
> *Fiction*. New Haven: Yale UP,     D4
> 1981.     P58
>
>
> '81 *MLA Bib.* 4: 1622

The sample bibliography card above contains not only all the information needed for the final bibliography (author's name, full title, and relevant publication information) but also information useful in conducting research: at the bottom, the source of the reference (*1981 MLA International Bibliography*, vol. 4, item 1622) and, in the upper right-hand corner, the call number indicated for the book in the library catalog.

Once you have a reference in hand, verify the publication information you have on your bibliography card and add any missing information that you will need for the final bibliography. For a book, check the author's name, title, subtitle (if any), edition (if relevant), the number of volumes, the city of publication, the publisher, and the year of publication. (This information normally appears on the title and copyright pages of the book.) For an article in a periodical, check the author's name, the title of the article, the title of the periodical, the date of publication, and the inclusive page numbers. If the article is in a scholarly journal, check the volume number as well. (Volume numbers and dates of publication normally appear on the title pages of periodicals.) Correct the information on the bibliography card if it disagrees with the publication facts obtained from the work itself.

If compiled with care and attention, the working bibliography will be invaluable to you throughout the preparation of your paper. It will, on the one hand, function as an efficient tool for finding and acquiring information and ideas and, on the other, provide all the information needed for the final bibliography of the paper.

## 1.5.  Taking notes

After you have verified the publication information for a source, the next step is to read and evaluate the material. Needless to say, you should not assume that something is truthful or trustworthy just because it is in print. Some material may be based on incorrect or outdated information, on poor logic, or on the author's own narrow opinions. Weigh what you read against your own knowledge and intelligence as well as against other treatments of the subject.

When you find material that you consider reliable and useful to your purpose, you will want to take notes on it. Although everyone agrees that note-taking is essential to research, probably no two researchers use exactly the same methods. Some take notes on a second set of index cards; others write in notebooks, beginning each new entry on a fresh page; still others favor loose-leaf or legal-size pages clipped together according to one system or another. Whatever your preference, take down first, at the very top of the page or card, the author's full name and the complete title—enough information to enable you to locate the corresponding bibliography card easily when you need it.

There are, generally speaking, three methods of note-taking: summary, paraphrase, and quotation. Summarize if you want to record only the general idea of large amounts of material. If you require detailed notes on specific sentences and passages, but not the exact wording, you may wish to paraphrase—that is, to restate the material in your own words. But, when you believe that some sentence or passage in its original wording might make an effective addition to your paper, transcribe that material exactly as it appears, word for word, comma for comma. Whenever you quote from a work, be sure to use quotation marks scrupulously in your notes to distinguish between verbatim quotation and summary or paraphrase. Keep an accurate record, preferably in the left-hand margin, of the page numbers of all material you summarize, paraphrase, or quote. When a quotation continues to another page, be careful to note where the page break occurs, since only a small portion of what you transcribe may ultimately find its way into your paper.

In taking notes, try to be both concise and thorough. Above all, however, strive for accuracy, not only in copying words for direct quotation but also in summarizing and paraphrasing authors' ideas. Careful note-taking will help you avoid the problem of plagiarism.

## 1.6.  Plagiarism

You may have heard the word "plagiarism" used in relation to lawsuits in the publishing and recording industries. You may also have had classroom discussions about academic plagiarism. Plagiarism is the act of using another person's ideas or expressions in your writing without acknowledging the source. The word comes from the Latin word *plagiarius* ("kidnapper"), and Alexander Lindey defines it as "the false assumption of authorship: the wrongful act of taking the product of another person's mind, and presenting it as one's own" (*Plagiarism and Originality* [New York: Harper, 1952] 2). In short, to plagiarize is to give the impression that you have written or thought something that you have in fact borrowed from someone else.

Plagiarism in student writing is often unintentional, as when an elementary school pupil, assigned to do a report on a certain topic, goes home and copies down, word for word, everything on the subject in an encyclopedia. Unfortunately, some students continue to use such "research methods" in high school and even in college without realizing that these practices constitute plagiarism. You may certainly use other persons' words and thoughts in your research paper, but you must acknowledge the authors.

Plagiarism often carries severe penalties, ranging from failure in a course to expulsion from school.

The most blatant form of plagiarism is to repeat as your own someone else's sentences, more or less verbatim. Suppose, for example, that you want to use the material in the following passage, which appears on page 906 in volume 1 of the *Literary History of the United States*:

The major concerns of Dickinson's poetry early and late, her "flood subjects," may be defined as the seasons and nature, death and a problematic afterlife, the kinds and phases of love, and poetry as the divine art.

If you write the following without any documentation, you have committed plagiarism:

The chief subjects of Emily Dickinson's poetry include nature and the seasons, death and the afterlife, the various types and stages of love, and poetry itself as a divine art.

But you may present the information if you credit the authors:

Gibson and Williams suggest that the chief subjects of Emily Dickinson's poetry include

nature, death, love, and poetry as a divine art
(1: 906).

The sentence and the parenthetical documentation at the end indicate the source, since the authors' names and the volume and page numbers refer the reader to the corresponding entry in the bibliography:

Gibson, William M., and Stanley T. Williams.

"Experiment in Poetry: Emily Dickinson and

Sidney Lanier." <u>Literary History of the</u>

<u>United States</u>. Ed. Robert E. Spiller et al.

4th ed. 2 vols. New York: Macmillan, 1974.

1: 899-916.

Other forms of plagiarism include repeating someone else's particularly apt phrase without appropriate acknowledgment, paraphrasing another person's argument as your own, and presenting another's line of thinking in the development of an idea as though it were your own. Two more examples follow:

### Original source

This, of course, raises the central question of this paper: What should we be doing? Research and training in the whole field of restructuring the world as an "ecotopia" (eco-, from *oikos*, household; -topia from *topos*, place, with implication of "eutopia"—"good place") will presumably be the goal. (From E. N. Anderson, Jr., "The Life and Culture of Ecotopia," *Reinventing Anthropology*, ed. Dell Hymes [1969; New York: Vintage-Random, 1974] 275.)

### Plagiarized in student writing
At this point in time humankind should be

attempting to create what we might call an

"ecotopia."

### Original source

Humanity faces a quantum leap forward. It faces the deepest social upheaval and creative restructuring of all time. Without clearly recognizing it, we are engaged in building a remarkable civilization from the ground up. This is the meaning of the Third Wave.

Until now the human race has undergone two great waves of change, each one largely obliterating earlier cultures or civilizations and replacing them with ways of life inconceivable to those who came before. The First Wave of change—the agricultural revolution—took thousands of years to play itself out. The Second Wave—the rise of industrial civilization—took a mere hundred years. Today history is even more accelerative, and it is likely that the Third Wave will sweep across history and complete itself in a few decades. (From Alvin Toffler, *The Third Wave* [1980; New York: Bantam, 1981] 10.)

### Plagiarized in student writing

There have been two revolutionary periods of

change in history: the agricultural revolution and

the industrial revolution.  The agricultural

revolution determined the course of history for

thousands of years; the industrial civilization

lasted about a century.  We are now on the

threshold of a new period of revolutionary change,

but this one may last for only a few decades.

In the first example, the writer borrowed a specific term ("ecotopia") without acknowledgment; in the second example, the writer presented another's line of thinking without giving that person credit. Once again, however, the students could have avoided the charge of plagiarism by rewording slightly and inserting appropriate parenthetical documentation.

At this point in time humankind should be

attempting to create what E. N. Anderson, Jr., has

called an "ecotopia" (275).

According to Alvin Toffler, there have been two

```
revolutionary periods of change in history: the

agricultural revolution and the industrial

revolution.  The agricultural revolution

determined the course of history for thousands of

years; the industrial civilization lasted about a

century.  We are now on the threshold of a new

period of revolutionary change, but this one may

last for only a few decades (10).
```

As before, the sentence and the parenthetical documentation in each revision identify the source of the borrowed material and refer the reader to the full description of the work in the bibliography at the end of the paper:

```
Anderson, E. N., Jr.  "The Life and Culture of

    Ecotopia."  Reinventing Anthropology.  Ed.

    Dell Hymes.  1969.  New York: Vintage-Random,

    1974.  264-81.

Toffler, Alvin.  The Third Wave.  1980.  New York:

    Bantam, 1981.
```

If you have any doubt about whether or not you are committing plagiarism, cite your source or sources.

## 1.7.  Outlining

When you have concluded your research for your paper, it is time to begin to shape the information you have at hand into a unified, coherent whole. A useful first step is to frame a thesis statement for your paper. In two or three sentences write down exactly what you wish to accomplish. Writing a thesis statement is a way of making sure that you do indeed know where you are heading, and it will help keep you on the right track as you plan and write. Many instructors require students to submit a thesis statement for approval some two or three weeks before the paper is due. If you have difficulty writing a thesis statement, consult your instructor. Since you have done research on the topic and presumably have some ideas about what you want to say, your instructor can often help you frame an appropriate thesis statement.

The following is an example of a thesis statement for a paper on the importance of using the library for writing a research paper.

```
Knowledge of the library is essential for writing

a research paper.  Making use of available

orientation programs and materials, the student

researcher should learn as much as possible about

the library's central catalog, the reference works

available, the various locations of materials, and

the services provided.  The more students know

about the library, the more successful their

research papers will be.
```

After you have framed a satisfactory thesis statement, you should prepare a preliminary outline for the paper. Like the thesis statement, the outline is an important intermediate step between the research and writing stages. It will help you organize your ideas and the accumulated research into a logical, fluent, and effective paper. Again, many instructors request that an outline be submitted either before or with the paper itself.

In preparing the preliminary outline, jot down your ideas for the paper, first, and then carefully review all your notes for additional ideas and supporting references. Next, read over what you have written down and delete everything that is irrelevant to the thesis statement or that would weaken the paper. Eliminating material is often painful since it is only natural to want to use everything you have collected and to impress your readers (especially teacher-readers) with all the work you have done and with all you now know on the subject. But you should fight these tendencies, for the inclusion of unhelpful, misleading, irrelevant, or repetitive material will detract from the effectiveness of the paper. In short, keep your thesis statement and your audience in mind. Include only the ideas and information that will help you accomplish what you have set out to do and that will interest and inform your readers, not confuse or bore them.

As you continue to read, reread, and think about the ideas and information you have decided to use, you will begin to see connections between various items, and certain patterns of organization will suggest themselves. Bring related material together under general headings, and arrange these sections so that one logically flows into another. Then order the subjects under each heading so that they, too, logically flow from one into the other. Finally, plan an effective introduction and a conclusion appropriate to the sequence you have worked out. Common organizing principles are time (useful for historical discussions), space (useful for some descriptions), or logic. A logical development may move from the general to the specific (e.g., from the problems of transportation to the disadvantages of travel by automobile) or from the specific to the general (e.g., from the disadvantages of travel by automobile to the problems of transportation).

In choosing an organizational plan, keep in mind the method or methods you will use in developing your paper. For example, do you plan somewhere in the paper to define, classify, or analyze something? to use descriptive details or give examples? to compare or contrast one thing with another? The procedures you intend to adopt will obviously influence the way you arrange your material, and they should be evident in your outline.

In general, then, make your outline as detailed as possible. It is a good idea to indicate, specifically and precisely, not only the methods of development but also the quotations and reference sources you will use. All this planning will take a good deal of time and thought, and you may well make several preliminary outlines before you arrive at the one you will follow. But the time and thought will be well spent. The more planning you do, the easier and more efficient the writing will be.

If the final outline is only for your use, its form will have little importance. If it is to be submitted, your instructor will probably discuss the various forms of outline—for example, the topic outline (which uses only short phrases throughout) and the sentence outline—and tell you which to use. Whatever the form, however, maintain it consistently.

The descending parts of an outline are normally labeled in the following order:

I.
   A.
      1.
         a.
            (1)
               (a)
               (b)
            (2)
         b.
      2.
   B.
II.

Logic requires that there be a "II" to complement a "I," a "B" to complement an "A," and so forth. The following sample is a topic outline of section 1.3.

### Using the Library

I.    Introduction--the importance of the library for the research paper

II.   Methods of learning about the library

    A.    Programs of orientation and instruction

        1.    Pamphlets, handbooks, other materials distributed by the library

        2.    Class visits, tours, lectures, courses

    B.    Books about the library (examples: Gates, Cook, Patterson, Baker)

III. The central catalog

    A.   Method of locating books in the catalog

        1.   Author

        2.   Title

        3.   Subject

    B.   Methods of arranging cards

        1.   Single catalog

        2.   Two or more catalogs

    C.   Systems of classification

        1.   Dewey Decimal system

        2.   Library of Congress system

    D.   Sample catalog cards

        1.   Author card

        2.   Title card

        3.   Subject card

IV. Reference works

    A.   Dictionaries, encyclopedias, other reference works

        1.   General works (dictionaries, encyclopedias, biographical works, yearbooks, atlases, gazetteers)

        2. Specialized dictionaries and encyclopedias (in alphabetical order: art, astronomy, etc.)

    B. Indexes, bibliographies, abstracts

        1. Indexes to periodicals (newspapers, magazines)

        2. Specialized bibliographies and indexes (in alphabetical order: art, biology, etc.)

        3. Abstracts (in alphabetical order: <u>Abstracts in Anthropology</u>, etc.)

**V.** Location of library materials

    A. Main collection

        1. Open shelves

        2. Closed stacks

    B. Special sections

        1. Folio-size books

        2. Reserved books

        3. Reference works

        4. Special collections

        5. Current periodicals, pamphlets, clippings, nonprint materials

VI.  Library services

  A.   Microforms: microfilm, microcard,

       microfiche

  B.   Computer assistance in research

       1.   Information storage systems

       2.   Retrieval systems

  C.   Other assistance (e.g., copying

       facilities, interlibrary loans)

VII. Conclusion--the importance of knowing about

     the library, its materials and services

## 1.8.  Writing drafts

Once you have your final outline in hand, you are ready to begin writing. But do not expect your first draft to be the finished product. The successful research paper is usually the culmination of a series of drafts.

Start off by trying to set down all your ideas in the order in which you want them to appear. Even though the writing may be hasty and fairly rough, the first draft should follow your outline very closely. You should then read over this raw material and try to refine it. Next, review the corrected draft and make further changes. Continue this process until you are satisfied that you have done the best you can in the time available.

In revising, you may add, eliminate, and rearrange material. If a section in the first draft seems unclear or sketchy, you may have to expand it by writing another sentence or two or even a new paragraph. Similarly, to improve the fluency and coherence of the paper, you may need to add transitions to show how one sentence relates to another or how one paragraph leads to the next. For the sake of unity and reader interest, you should delete any material that is irrelevant, unimportant, repetitive, or dull and unnecessary. If the presentation of ideas seems illogical or confusing, you may find that you can clarify by rearranging phrases, clauses, sentences, or paragraphs.

In later drafts you should concern yourself with the more mechanical kinds of revision. For example, strive for more precise and economical wording. Try, in addition, to vary your sentence patterns as well as your choice of words. Finally, correct all technical errors, using a standard writing guide to check punctuation, grammar, and usage and consulting a standard dictionary to check the spelling and meaning of words. Your last draft, retyped, carefully proofread, and corrected, is the text of your research paper.

## 1.9.  Guides to writing

Effective writing depends as much on clarity and readability as on content. The organization and development of your ideas, the unity and coherence of your presentation, and your command of sentence structure, grammar, and diction are all important considerations, as are the mechanics of writing—capitalization, spelling, punctuation, and so on. The key to successful communication is using the right language. In all writing, the challenge is to find the words, phrases, clauses, sentences, and paragraphs that express your thoughts and ideas precisely and that make them interesting to others.

There is still another aspect of language to consider. In recent years, writers, teachers, and publishers have become increasingly concerned about its social connotations. The careful writer avoids statements that reflect or imply unsubstantiated generalizations about a person's age, economic class, national origin, sexual orientation, political or religious beliefs, race, or sex. Your language, in other words, should not suggest bias or prejudice toward any group. For example, many writers no longer use "he" to refer to someone of unspecified sex—"a doctor" or "an executive," say—lest readers infer that the statement can apply only to a man. For advice on current practices, consult your instructor or one of the more recent guides listed below.

A good dictionary is an essential tool in writing. Your instructor can recommend a standard American dictionary such as *The American College Dictionary, The American Heritage Dictionary of the English Language, The Random House Dictionary of the English Language,* or *Webster's New Collegiate Dictionary.* Because dictionaries vary in matters such as hyphenation and the preferred spelling of words, you should, to maintain consistency, use the same one throughout your paper.

You should also keep on hand a reliable guide to writing. Your instructor can help you choose one of the many available. A selected list of writing guides appears below, classified under three headings: hand-books of composition, dictionaries of usage, and books on style.

### Handbooks of composition

Baker, Sheridan. *The Complete Stylist and Handbook*. 3rd ed. New York: Harper, 1984.

————. *The Practical Stylist*. 5th ed. New York: Harper, 1981.

Bell, James K., and Adrian A. Cohn. *Handbook of Grammar, Style, and Usage*. 3rd ed. New York: Macmillan, 1981.

Corbett, Edward P. J. *The Little Rhetoric and Handbook with Readings*. Glenview: Scott, 1983.

Crews, Frederick. *The Random House Handbook*. 3rd ed. New York: Random, 1980.

Ebbitt, Wilma R., and David R. Ebbitt. *Writer's Guide and Index to English*. 7th ed. Glenview: Scott, 1981.

Elsbree, Langdon, et al. *Heath Handbook of Composition*. 10th ed. Lexington: Heath, 1981.

Fear, David E., and Gerald J. Schiffhorst. *Short English Handbook*. 2nd ed. Glenview: Scott, 1982.

Fowler, H. Ramsey. *The Little, Brown Handbook*. 2nd ed. Boston: Little, 1983.

Gorrell, Robert M., and Charlton Laird. *Modern English Handbook*. 6th ed. Englewood Cliffs: Prentice, 1976.

Guth, Hans P. *Words and Ideas: A Handbook for College Writing*. 5th ed. Belmont: Wadsworth, 1980.

Heffernan, James A. W., and John E. Lincoln. *Writing: A College Handbook*. New York: Norton, 1982.

Hodges, John C., and Mary E. Whitten. *Harbrace College Handbook*. 9th ed. New York: Harcourt, 1982.

Irmscher, William F. *The Holt Guide to English: A Contemporary Handbook of Rhetoric, Language, and Literature*. 3rd ed. New York: Holt, 1981.

Leggett, Glenn C., David Mead, and William Charvat. *Prentice-Hall Handbook for Writers*. 8th ed. Englewood Cliffs: Prentice, 1982.

McCrimmon, James M. *Writing with a Purpose: Short Edition*. Boston: Houghton, 1980.

Watkins, Floyd C., and William B. Dillingham. *Practical English Handbook*. 6th ed. Boston: Houghton, 1982.

### Dictionaries of usage

Bernstein, Theodore. *The Careful Writer: A Modern Guide to English Usage*. New York: Atheneum, 1965.

Bryant, Margaret M. *Current American Usage: How Americans Say It and Write It*. New York: Funk, 1962.

Copperud, Roy H. *American Usage: The Consensus.* New York: Van Nostrand, 1970.

Evans, Bergen, and Cornelia Evans. *Dictionary of Contemporary American Usage.* New York: Random, 1957.

Follett, Wilson. *Modern American Usage: A Guide.* Ed. Jacques Barzun. New York: Hill, 1966.

Fowler, Henry W. *A Dictionary of Modern English Usage.* Ed. Ernest Gowers. 2nd ed. New York: Oxford UP, 1965.

Nicholson, Margaret. *A Dictionary of American-English Usage Based on Fowler's* Modern English Usage. New York: Oxford UP, 1957.

### Books on style

Beardsley, Monroe C. *Thinking Straight: Principles of Reasoning for Readers and Writers.* 4th ed. Englewood Cliffs: Prentice, 1975.

Cowan, Gregory, and Elisabeth McPherson. *Plain English Please.* 4th ed. New York: Random, 1976.

Eastman, Richard M. *Style: Writing as the Discovery of Outlook.* 2nd ed. New York: Oxford UP, 1978.

Elbow, Peter. *Writing with Power: Techniques for Mastering the Writing Process.* New York: Oxford UP, 1981.

———. *Writing without Teachers.* New York: Oxford UP, 1975.

Gibson, Walker. *Tough, Sweet, and Stuffy: An Essay on Modern American Prose Styles.* Bloomington: Indiana UP, 1966.

Gowers, Ernest. *The Complete Plain Words.* Ed. Bruce Fraser. 2nd ed. Baltimore: Penguin, 1975.

Lanham, Richard A. *Style: An Anti-Textbook.* New Haven: Yale UP, 1974.

Smith, Charles K. *Styles and Structures: Alternative Approaches to Student Writing.* New York: Norton, 1974.

Strunk, William, Jr., and E. B. White. *The Elements of Style.* 3rd ed. New York: Macmillan, 1979.

White, Edward M. *The Writer's Control of Tone.* New York: Norton, 1970.

Williams, Joseph M. *Style: Ten Lessons in Clarity and Grace.* Glenview: Scott, 1981.

# 2 MECHANICS OF WRITING

Although the scope of this book precludes a detailed discussion of grammar, usage, style, and related aspects of writing, this chapter addresses mechanical questions that commonly arise in research writing:

1. Spelling
2. Punctuation
3. Names of persons
4. Numbers
5. Titles in the research paper
6. Quotations
7. Languages other than English

## 2.1. Spelling

### 2.1.1. Consistency

Spelling, including hyphenation, should be consistent throughout the research paper—except in quotations, which must retain the spelling of the original. To ensure accuracy and consistency, always adopt the spelling that your dictionary gives first in an entry.

### 2.1.2. Word division

Avoid dividing words at the end of a line. If the word you are about to type will obviously not fit on the line, you may leave the line short and begin the word on the next line. To divide a word, consult your dictionary about where the break should occur.

### 2.1.3. Foreign words

If you are quoting from a foreign language, reproduce all accents and other marks exactly as they appear in the original: école, frère, tête, leçon, Fähre, año. If your typewriter does not have these marks, write them in by hand.

## 2.2. Punctuation

### 2.2.1. Consistency

The primary purpose of punctuation is to ensure the clarity and readability of your writing. Although punctuation is, to some extent, a matter of personal preference, there are many required uses, and while certain practices are optional, consistency is mandatory. Be sure to use the same punctuation in parallel situations.

## 2.2.2. Apostrophes

Apostrophes indicate contractions (rarely acceptable in research papers) and possessives. To form the possessive of a singular noun, add an apostrophe and an *s* (the accountant's ledger, television's influence); to form the possessive of a plural noun ending in *s*, add only an apostrophe (the accountants' ledgers, the soldiers' weapons). Some irregular plurals require an apostrophe and an *s* (the media's role, women's studies). All singular proper nouns, including the names of persons and places, form their possessives in the same manner (Mars's wrath, Camus's novel, Kansas's weather, Dickens's popularity, *but* the Dickenses' economic problems).

Apostrophes are also used to form the plurals of letters (*p*'s and *q*'s; *A*'s, *B*'s, *C*'s). But do not use apostrophes to form the plurals of abbreviations or numbers (PhDs, MAs, 1960s, fours, 780s, SATs in the 780s).

## 2.2.3. Colons

A colon indicates that what follows will be an example, explanation, or elaboration of what has just been said. Do not use a colon where a semicolon should be used (see 2.2.12).

`He was in the midst of a dilemma about his career:`

`he wanted to stay, but he preferred the job in`

`Florida.`

but

`He was in the midst of a dilemma about his career;`

`he also felt overworked.`

Colons are commonly used to introduce quotations (see 2.6.2–3, 2.6.6) and to separate titles from subtitles (*Anatomy of Criticism: Four Essays*).

In references and bibliographic citations, colons separate volume numbers from page numbers (3: 81–112), the city of publication from the name of the book publisher (New York: Norton, 1983), and the date of publication from the page numbers of an article in a periodical (15 Feb. 1980: 10–15). Skip only one space after a colon, never two.

## 2.2.4. Commas

Commas are required between items in a series, between coordinate adjectives, before coordinating conjunctions joining independent clauses, around parenthetical elements, and after fairly long phrases or clauses preceding the main clauses of sentences.

**The experience demanded blood, sweat, and tears.**

**We listened to an absorbing, frightening account**

**of the event.**

**Congress passed the bill by a wide margin, and the**

**president signed it into law.**

**The invention, the first in a series during that**

**decade, completely changed people's lives.**

**After carefully studying all the available**

**historical documents and personal writings,**

**scholars could come to no definitive conclusion.**

Commas are also used in dates (June 23, 1983; but 23 June 1983), names (Cal Ripken, Jr., and Walter J. Ong, SJ; but John Hayes III), and addresses (Rosemary Brady of 160 Carroll Street, Brooklyn, New York, visited her sister in Brooklyn, Maryland). A comma and a dash are never used together. If the context requires a comma (as it does here), the comma follows a closing parenthesis. (See 2.6.6 for commas with quotations; see chs. 4 and 5 for the uses of the comma in documentation and bibliography.)

## 2.2.5.  Dashes

To indicate a dash in typing, use two hyphens, with no space before, between, or after. Do not overuse dashes, substituting them for other punctuation marks. The dash may be used around parenthetical elements that represent a break in the flow of thought, around parenthetical elements that require a number of internal commas, and before a summarizing appositive.

```
The rapid spread of the disease--the number of

reported cases doubled each six months--helped

create the sense of panic.
```

```
Many twentieth-century American writers--Faulkner,

Capote, Styron, Welty, to name only a few--come

from the South.
```

```
Computer chips, integrated circuits, bits, and

bytes--these new terms baffled yet intrigued.
```

## 2.2.6. Exclamation marks

Except in direct quotation, exclamation marks should generally not be used in research writing.

## 2.2.7. Hyphens

Hyphens are used to connect numbers indicating a range (1-20) and also to form some types of compound words, particularly compound words that precede the words they modify (a well-established policy, a first-rate study). Hyphens also join prefixes to capitalized words (post-Renaissance) and link pairs of coequal nouns (poet-priest, scholar-athlete). Many other word combinations, however, are written as one word (hardworking employees, storytelling) or as two or more words (social security tax, ad hoc committee). Note especially that adverbs ending in "ly" do not form hyphenated compounds (a wildly successful debut). Consult a standard dictionary or writing manual for guidance on the hyphenation of specific terms.

## 2.2.8.  Italics

Some titles are italicized (underlined in typing), as are letters, words, or phrases cited as linguistic examples, words referred to as words, and foreign words in an English text. The numerous exceptions to this last rule include quotations entirely in another language; non-English titles of short works (poems, short stories, essays, articles), which are placed in quotation marks and not underlined; proper names; and foreign words anglicized through frequent use. Since American English rapidly naturalizes words, use a dictionary to decide whether a foreign expression requires italics. Adopted foreign words, abbreviations, and phrases commonly not underlined include cliché, détente, e.g., et al., etc., genre, hubris, laissez-faire, raison d'être, roman à clef, tête-à-tête, and versus.

Italics for emphasis (I *never* said that) should be used sparingly, since this device rapidly loses its effectiveness. It is rarely appropriate in research writing.

## 2.2.9.  Parentheses

Parentheses enclose parenthetical remarks that break too sharply with the surrounding text to be enclosed in commas. Parentheses sometimes dictate a greater separation than dashes would, but often either set of marks is acceptable, the choice depending on the other punctuation required in the context. Parentheses are used around documentation within the text (see 5.2) and around publication information in notes (see 5.8.3).

## 2.2.10.  Periods

Periods end declarative sentences, notes, and complete blocks of information in bibliographic citations. Periods between numbers indicate related parts of a work (e.g., 1.2 for act 1, scene 2).

The period follows a parenthesis that falls at the end of a sentence. It goes within the parenthesis when the enclosed element is independent (see, not this sentence, but the next). (For the use of periods with ellipsis points, see 2.6.4.)

## 2.2.11.  Quotation marks

Quotation marks should enclose quoted material (see 2.6), certain titles (see 2.5.3), and words or phrases purposely misused or used in a special sense (e.g., their "benefactor" was ultimately responsible for their downfall).

Double quotation marks are used around parenthetical translations of words or phrases from another language, but single quotation marks are used for definitions or translations that appear without intervening punctuation (*ainsi* 'thus').

## 2.2.12.  Semicolons

Semicolons are used between items in series when some of the items require internal commas, between closely related independent clauses not joined by coordinating conjunctions, and before coordinating conjunctions linking independent clauses that require a number of internal commas.

In one day the indefatigable candidate campaigned in Vail, Colorado; Columbus, Ohio; Nashville, Tennessee; and Teaneck, New Jersey.

On the one hand, demand is steadily decreasing; on the other, production keeps inexplicably increasing.

The overture begins with a brooding, mournful passage in the strings and woodwinds, one of the composer's most passionate statements; but the piece concludes with a burst of lively, spirited, almost comic music in the brass and percussion.

For the use of semicolons in parenthetical documentation and bibliography, see chapters 4 and 5.

## 2.2.13.  Slashes

Slashes (or virgules) are used to separate lines of poetry (see 2.6.3), elements in dates expressed exclusively in digits (e.g., 2/12/84), and, occasionally, alternative words (and/or). Use a space before and after the slash only when separating lines of poetry.

## 2.2.14. Square brackets

Square brackets are used for a parenthesis within a parenthesis where necessary to avoid two pairs of parentheses, to enclose interpolations in quotations (see 2.6.5), and to indicate missing or unverified data in documentation (see 4.5.25). Insert square brackets by hand if they are not on your typewriter.

# 2.3. Names of persons

## 2.3.1. First and subsequent uses of names

The first time you use a person's name in the text of your research paper, state it fully and accurately, exactly as it appears in the source you have read.

`Arthur George Rust, Jr.`

`Victoria M. Sackville-West`

Do not change "Arthur George Rust, Jr." to "Arthur George Rust" or drop the hyphen in "Victoria M. Sackville-West." In subsequent uses of the name, you may give the person's last name only (Sackville-West)— unless, of course, you refer to two or more persons with the same last name—or give the most common form of the person's name (e.g., Michelangelo for Michelangelo Buonarotti; Surrey for Henry Howard, earl of Surrey; Disraeli for Benjamin Disraeli, first earl of Beaconsfield). In some languages (e.g., Chinese, Hungarian, Japanese, Korean, and Vietnamese), surnames precede given names; consult reference works for guidance with these names. For rules concerning names of persons in other languages, see 2.7.

## 2.3.2. Titles of persons

In general, do not use formal titles (Dr., Miss, Mr., Mrs., Ms., Professor, etc.) in referring to persons, living or dead: Churchill, *not* Mr. Churchill; Einstein, *not* Professor Einstein. A few women in history are traditionally known by their married names (e.g., Mrs. Humphry Ward, Mme de Staël). Otherwise, treat women's names the same as men's.

| First use | Thereafter |
|---|---|
| Emily Dickinson | Dickinson (not Miss Dickinson) |
| Harriet Beecher Stowe | Stowe (not Mrs. Stowe) |
| Margaret Mead | Mead (not Ms. Mead) |

### 2.3.3. Names of authors and fictional characters

It is common and acceptable to use simplified names of famous authors (Vergil for Publius Vergilius Maro, Dante for Dante Alighieri). Pseudonyms should be treated as ordinary names.

Molière (Jean-Baptiste Poquelin)
Voltaire (François-Marie Arouet)
George Sand (Amandine-Aurore-Lucie Dupin)
George Eliot (Mary Ann Evans)
Mark Twain (Samuel Clemens)
Stendhal (Marie-Henri Beyle)
Novalis (Friedrich von Hardenberg)

Fictional characters should be referred to as they are in the work of fiction. Full names need not always be given, and titles need not be omitted (e.g., Dr. Jekyll).

## 2.4. Numbers

### 2.4.1. Arabic numerals

Although there are still a few well-established uses for roman numerals (see 2.4.7), common practice today is to use arabic numerals to represent virtually all numbers. If your typewriter does not have the number "1," use a small letter el ("l"), not capital "I," for the arabic numeral.

### 2.4.2. Use of words or numerals

In general, write as words all numbers from one to nine and write as numerals all numbers 10 and over (about 500 years ago). But never begin a sentence with a numeral (Five hundred years ago . . .). Always use numerals with abbreviations and symbols (6 lbs., 8KB, 4 p.m., $9, 3%, 2″) and in addresses (5 13th Avenue), dates (1 April 1984), decimal fractions (8.3), and page references (page 7). For very large numbers you may use a combination of numerals and words: 4.5 million. Related numbers must be expressed in the same style: 5 out of 217 British troops, 3 automobiles and 12 trucks, from 1 billion to 1.2 billion.

In discussions involving infrequent use of numbers, you may spell out numbers that can be written in no more than two words and represent other numbers by numerals (one, thirty-six, ninety-nine, one hundred, fifteen hundred, two thousand, three million; but 2½, 101, 137, and 1,275).

## 2.4.3. Commas in numbers

Commas are usually placed between the third and fourth digits from the right, the sixth and seventh, and so on.

```
1,000    20,000    7,654,321
```

Exceptions to this practice include page and line numbers, addresses, and four-digit year numbers. Commas are added in longer year numbers.

```
On page 3322. . . .

At 4132 Broadway. . . .

In 1984. . . .

In 20,000 BC. . . .
```

## 2.4.4. Percentages and amounts of money

Treat percentages and amounts of money as other numbers: use numerals with the appropriate symbols (1%, 45%, 100%, $5.35, $35, $2,000, 68¢). In discussions involving infrequent use of numbers, you may spell out percentages and amounts of money if you can do so in no more than two words (five dollars, forty-five percent, two thousand dollars, sixty-eight cents). Do not combine spelled forms of numbers with symbols.

## 2.4.5. Dates

Be consistent in writing dates: use either "22 July 1986" or "July 22, 1986," but not both. (If you begin with the month, be sure to add a comma after the day and also after the year, unless another punctuation mark goes there, such as a period or a question mark.) Do not use a comma between month and year: August 1984.

Spell out centuries in lowercase letters (the twentieth century) and hyphenate them as adjectives (eighteenth-century thought, nineteenth- and twentieth-century literature). Decades are usually written out without capitalization (the eighties), but it is becoming acceptable to express them in figures: the 1980s or the '80s.

"BC" follows the year, but "AD" precedes it: 19 BC, AD 565. (Some writers use "BCE," before the Common Era, and "CE," Common Era.)

## 2.4.6. Inclusive numbers

In indicating a range of numbers, give the second number in full for numbers through 99: 2–3, 10–12, 21–48, 89–99. For larger numbers, give only the last two digits of the second number, unless more are necessary: 96–101, 103–04, 395–401, 923–1003, 1003–05, 1608–774. In giving a range of years, write both in full unless they are within the same century: 1898–1901, 1898–99.

## 2.4.7. Roman numerals

Use capital roman numerals for primary divisions of an outline and for individuals in a series: Henry VIII, John Paul II, Elizabeth II. Use lowercase roman numerals for citing pages of a book that are so numbered (e.g., the pages in a preface). Your instructor may also prefer that you use roman numerals to designate acts and scenes of plays: "In *Othello* IV.ii we begin to see that. . . ."

# 2.5. Titles in the research paper

## 2.5.1. Capitalization and punctuation

Always take the title from the title page, not from the cover or from the top of each page. Do not reproduce any unusual typographical characteristics, such as all capital letters or the uncommon use of lowercase letters: MODERNISM & NEGRITUDE should appear as *Modernism and Negritude*; BERNARD BERENSON The Making of a Connoisseur as *Bernard Berenson: The Making of a Connoisseur*; Turner's early sketchbooks as *Turner's Early Sketchbooks*.

The rules for capitalizing titles are strict. In both titles and subtitles, capitalize the first words, the last words, and all principal words, including those that follow hyphens in compound terms. Therefore, capitalize nouns, pronouns, verbs, adjectives, and adverbs but not articles (a, an, the), prepositions introducing phrases (e.g., in, to, of, before), coordinating conjunctions (and, or, but, nor, for), or the *to* in infinitives, when such words fall in the middle of the title. Unless the title itself has ending punctuation, use a colon and a space to separate a title and a subtitle. Include other punctuation only if it is part of the title.

Death of a Salesman

The Teaching of Spanish in English-Speaking

Countries

<u>Storytelling and Mythmaking: Images from Film and</u>

  <u>Literature</u>

<u>What Is Literature?</u>

<u>Whose Music? A Sociology of Musical Language</u>

<u>Where Did You Go? Out. What Did You Do?</u>

  <u>Nothing.</u>

"Ode to a Nightingale"

"Italian Literature before Dante"

"What Americans Stand For: Two Views"

"Why Fortinbras?"

When the first line of a poem serves as the title or part of the title, however, reproduce the line exactly as it appears in print.

For rules concerning capitalization in languages other than English, see 2.7.

## 2.5.2.  Underlined titles

To indicate titles in your text, either underline them or enclose them in quotation marks. In general, underline the titles of works published independently and use quotation marks for the titles of works published within larger works (e.g., the article "Crime Rate Declines" appears in the newspaper the *New York Times*).

Titles to be underlined include the names of books, plays, long poems published as books, pamphlets, periodicals (newspapers, magazines, and journals), films, radio and television programs, record albums, ballets, operas, instrumental musical compositions (except those identified simply by form, number, and key), paintings, works of sculpture, and ships, aircraft, and spacecraft. In the following examples note that the underlining is not broken between words. While it is not necessary to underline the spaces between words, a continuous line is easier to type, and it guards against the error of failing to underline the punctuation within a title.

<u>David Copperfield</u> (published book)

<u>As You Like It</u> (play)

<u>The Waste Land</u> (long poem)

<u>New Jersey Driver Manual</u> (pamphlet)

<u>Wall Street Journal</u> (newspaper)

<u>Time</u> (magazine)

<u>Sounder</u> (film)

<u>Star Trek</u> (television program)

<u>Robert Frost Reads His Poetry</u> (record album)

<u>Giselle</u> (ballet)

<u>Rigoletto</u> (opera)

Berlioz's <u>Symphonie fantastique</u> (instrumental musical
     composition identified by name)

Beethoven's Symphony no. 7 in A (instrumental musical
     composition identified by form, number, and key)

Chagall's <u>I and My Village</u> (painting)

Bernini's <u>Ecstasy of St. Teresa</u> (sculpture)

HMS <u>Vanguard</u> (ship)

<u>Spirit of St. Louis</u> (aircraft)


## 2.5.3. Titles in quotation marks

Enclose in quotation marks, and do not underline, the titles of articles, essays, short stories, short poems, chapters of books, and individual episodes of radio and television programs—all works that appear

within larger works. Also use quotation marks for songs and for unpublished works, such as lectures and speeches.

"Sharp Rise in Unemployment" (article in a newspaper)

"Sources of Energy in the Twenty-First Century"
(article in a magazine)

"The Writer's Audience Is Always a Fiction" (article
in a scholarly journal)

"Etruscan" (encyclopedia article)

"The Fiction of Langston Hughes" (essay in a book)

"Young Goodman Brown" (short story)

"Kubla Khan" (poem)

"Summertime" (song)

"Italian Literature before Dante" (chapter in a book)

"The Trouble with Tribbles" (episode of the television
program *Star Trek*)

"Preparing for a Successful Interview" (lecture)

## 2.5.4. Titles within titles

If a title indicated by quotation marks appears within an underlined title, retain the quotation marks. If a title indicated by underlining appears within a title enclosed by quotation marks, retain the underlining.

<u>"Young Goodman Brown" and Hawthorne's Puritan</u>

<u>Heritage</u> (book)

**"<u>As You Like It</u> as a Pastoral Poem"** (article)

When a title normally indicated by quotation marks appears within another title requiring quotation marks, the shorter title is given single quotation marks.

**"An Interpretation of Coleridge's 'Kubla Khan'"**

(article)

When a normally underlined title appears within another underlined title, the short title appears neither underlined nor in quotation marks.

**<u>Approaches to Teaching Dickens'</u> David Copperfield**

(book)

## 2.5.5.  Exceptions

The convention of using underlining or quotation marks to indicate titles does not apply to sacred writings (including all books and versions of the Bible); names of series, editions, and societies; descriptive words or phrases used instead of an actual title; and names of courses. None of these is underlined or put within quotation marks.

**Sacred writings**

| | |
|---|---|
| Bible | Gospels |
| King James Version | Talmud |
| Old Testament | Koran |
| Genesis | Upanishads |

**Series**

Bollingen Series

University of North Carolina Studies in

Comparative Literature

Masterpiece Theatre

**Editions**

New Variorum Edition of Shakespeare

Centenary Edition of the Works of Nathaniel

  Hawthorne

**Societies**

American Medical Association

Renaissance Society of America

**Descriptive words or phrases**

Roosevelt's first inaugural address

**Courses**

Introduction to Calculus

Anthropology 102

The divisions of a book or a literary work are also not underlined or put within quotation marks; they are lowercased when used in the text:

| | |
|---|---|
| preface | chapter 2 |
| introduction | act 4 |
| bibliography | scene 7 |
| appendix | stanza 20 |
| index | canto 32 |

## 2.5.6.  Shortened titles

If you cite a title often in the text of your paper, you may, after stating the title in full at least once, use thereafter only a shortened title (preferably a familiar or obvious one) or an abbreviation: "Nightingale" for "Ode to a Nightingale"; FCC for Federal Communications Commission. (For standard abbreviations of literary and religious works, see 6.7.)

# 2.6.  Quotations

## 2.6.1.  Use of quotations

While quotations are a common and often effective feature of a research paper, use them selectively. Quote only words, phrases, lines, and passages that are particularly interesting, vivid, unique, or apt, and keep all quotations as brief as possible. Overquotation can bore your readers and might lead them to conclude that you are neither an original thinker nor a skillful writer.

In general, a quotation—whether a word, phrase, sentence, or more—should correspond exactly to its source in spelling, capitalization, and interior punctuation. If you change it in any way, make the alteration clear to the reader, following the rules and recommendations explained below.

## 2.6.2.  Prose

Unless special emphasis is required, prose quotations of not more than four typed lines should be placed in quotation marks and incorporated within the text.

```
"It was the best of times, it was the worst of

times," wrote Charles Dickens of the eighteenth

century.
```

Remember, though, that you need not always reproduce complete sentences. Sometimes you may want to quote just a word or phrase as part of your sentence.

```
For Charles Dickens the eighteenth century was

both "the best of times" and "the worst of times."
```

You may put a quotation at the beginning, middle, or end of your sentence or, for the sake of variety or better style, divide it by your own words.

```
Joseph Conrad writes of the company manager in
```

<u>Heart of Darkness</u>, "He was obeyed, yet he inspired

neither love nor fear, nor even respect."

or

"He was obeyed," writes Conrad of the company

manager in <u>Heart of Darkness</u>, "yet he inspired

neither love nor fear, nor even respect."

If you wish to use a quotation of more than four typed lines, set it off from your text by beginning a new line, indenting ten spaces from the left margin, and typing it double-spaced, without adding quotation marks. A colon generally introduces a quotation displayed in this way, though sometimes the context may require a different mark of punctuation, or none at all. If you are quoting only a single paragraph, or part of one, do not indent the first line more than the rest.

At the conclusion of <u>Lord of the Flies</u> Ralph and

the other boys realize the horror of their

actions:

> The tears began to flow and sobs shook
>
> him.  He gave himself up to them now for
>
> the first time on the island; great,
>
> shuddering spasms of grief that seemed
>
> to wrench his whole body.  His voice
>
> rose under the black smoke before the
>
> burning wreckage of the island; and
>
> infected by that emotion, the other
>
> little boys began to shake and sob too.

```
And in the middle of them, with filthy

body, matted hair, and unwiped nose,

Ralph wept for the end of

innocence. . . .
```

In quoting two or more paragraphs, indent the first line of each paragraph an additional three spaces. If, however, the first sentence quoted does not begin a paragraph in the source, do not indent it the additional three spaces. Indent only the first line of the following paragraph.

## 2.6.3.   Poetry

Unless unusual emphasis is required, a verse quotation of a single line or part of a line should appear within quotation marks as part of your text. You may also incorporate two or three lines in this way, using a slash with a space on each side (/) to separate them.

```
In Shakespeare's Julius Caesar, Antony says of

Brutus, "This was the noblest Roman of them all."


In Julius Caesar, Antony begins his famous speech:

"Friends, Romans, countrymen, lend me your

ears; / I come to bury Caesar, not to praise him."
```

Verse quotations of more than three lines should begin on a new line. Unless the quotation involves unusual spacing, indent each line ten spaces from the left margin and double-space between lines, adding no quotation marks that do not appear in the original. If the lines quoted are so long that a ten-space indentation would make the page look unbalanced, you may indent fewer than ten spaces from the margin. And if the spatial arrangement of the original, including indentation and spacing within and between lines, is unusual, it should be reproduced as accurately as possible.

```
E. E. Cummings concludes the poem with this vivid
```

description of a carefree scene, reinforced by the

carefree form of the lines themselves:

                it's

                spring

                and

                      the

                            goat-footed


                balloonMan          whistles

                far

                and

                wee

A quotation that begins in the middle of the line of verse should be reproduced in that way and not shifted to the left margin.

It is in act 2 of <u>As You Like It</u> that Jaques is

given the speech that many think contains a

glimpse of Shakespeare's conception of drama:

                      All the world's a stage

            And all the men and women merely players:

            They have their exits and their entrances;

            And one man in his time plays many parts,

            His acts being seven ages.

```
Jaques then proceeds to enumerate and analyze

these ages.
```

## 2.6.4. Ellipsis

When you wish to omit a word, phrase, sentence, or paragraph from a quoted passage, you should be guided by two principles: (1) fairness to the author quoted and (2) the grammatical integrity of your own writing. If you quote only a word or a phrase, it will be obvious that you have left out some of the original sentence.

```
In his inaugural address, John F. Kennedy spoke of

a "new frontier."
```

But if omitting material from the original leaves a quotation that appears to be a sentence, or a series of sentences, you must use ellipsis points, or spaced periods, to indicate that your quotation does not completely reproduce the original.

For ellipsis *within* a sentence, use three periods ( ... ) with a space before and after each period.

### Original

Medical thinking, trapped in the theory of astral influences, stressed air as the communicator of disease, ignoring sanitation or visible carriers. (From Barbara W. Tuchman, *A Distant Mirror: The Calamitous Fourteenth Century* [1978; New York: Ballantine, 1979] 101–02.)

### Quoted with ellipsis in the middle

```
In seeking causes for plagues in the Middle Ages,

as Barbara W. Tuchman writes, "Medical thinking

. . . stressed air as the communicator of disease,

ignoring sanitation or visible carriers."
```

### Quoted with ellipsis in the middle, with parenthetical reference

```
In seeking causes for plagues in the Middle Ages,
```

as Barbara W. Tuchman writes, "Medical thinking

. . . stressed air as the communicator of disease,

ignoring sanitation or visible carriers" (101-02).

When the ellipsis coincides with the end of your sentence, use three spaced periods following a sentence period—that is, four periods, with no space before the first.

**Quoted with ellipsis at the end**

In seeking causes for plagues in the Middle Ages,

as Barbara W. Tuchman writes, "Medical thinking,

trapped in the theory of astral influences,

stressed air as the communicator of

disease. . . ."

If a parenthetical reference follows the ellipsis at the end of your sentence, use three spaced periods and place the sentence period after the final parenthesis.

**Quoted with ellipsis at the end, followed by parenthetical reference**

In seeking causes for plagues in the Middle Ages,

as Barbara W. Tuchman writes, "Medical thinking,

trapped in the theory of astral influences,

stressed air as the communicator of disease . . ."

(101-02).

Four periods may also be used to indicate the omission of a whole sentence or more, or even of a paragraph or more. Remember, however, that grammatically complete sentences must both precede and follow the four periods.

**Original**

Presidential control reached its zenith under Andrew Jackson, the extent of whose attention to the press even before he became a candidate is suggested by the fact that he subscribed to twenty newspapers. Jackson was never content to have only one organ grinding out his tune. For a time, the *United States Telegraph* and the *Washington Globe* were almost equally favored as party organs, and there were fifty-seven journalists on the government payroll. (From William L. Rivers, *The Mass Media: Reporting, Writing, Editing*, 2nd ed. [New York: Harper, 1975] 7.)

**Quoted with omission of a complete sentence**

In discussing the historical relationship between politics and the press, William L. Rivers notes, "Presidential control reached its zenith under Andrew Jackson. . . . For a time, the <u>United States Telegraph</u> and the <u>Washington Globe</u> were almost equally favored as party organs, and there were fifty-seven journalists on the government payroll" (7).

## 2.6.5. Other alterations of sources

Occasionally, you may decide that a quotation will be unclear or confusing to your reader unless you provide supplementary information. While you may add material to a quoted source, just as you may omit it, you should keep such contributions to a minimum and make sure to distinguish them from the original, usually through a brief explanation in either parentheses or square brackets.

An explanation that does not go within the quotation may appear in parentheses immediately after the closing quotation mark—for example, an indication that you have underlined words for emphasis.

Lincoln specifically advocated a government "<u>for</u> the people" (emphasis added).

Without the parenthetical addition, readers would assume that the word underlined in the quotation is italicized in the original. Sometimes it may also be necessary to use "sic" (Latin for "thus" or "so") in parentheses following a quotation to assure readers that the quotation is accurate even though the spelling or logic might lead them to think otherwise.

**The student referred to "Imitations of Immorality"**

**(sic) as one of Wordsworth's famous poems.**

If your comment or explanation goes inside the quotation, then the addition must appear within square brackets, not parentheses. (Since some typewriters do not include square brackets, you may have to insert them by hand.)

**The title of the student's paper was "My**

**Interpretation of 'Imitations of Immorality'**

**[sic]."**

Similarly, if a pronoun seems unclear in a quotation, you may follow it immediately with an identification in square brackets.

**Why, she would hang on him [Hamlet's father]**

**As if increase of appetite had grown**

**By what it fed on. . . .**

The accuracy of quotations in research writing is extremely important. They must reproduce the original exactly. Unless indicated in brackets, liberties must not be taken with the spelling or the punctuation of the source. In short, you must construct a clear, grammatically correct sentence that allows you to introduce or incorporate a quotation with complete accuracy. Alternatively, you can paraphrase the original and quote only fragments, which may be easier to integrate into the text. Methods vary, as the following example shows.

### Original

Moralists have unanimously agreed, that unless virtue be nursed by liberty, it will never attain due strength—and what they say of man I extend to mankind, insisting that in all cases morals be fixed on immutable principles; and, that the being cannot be termed rational or virtuous, who obeys any authority, but that of reason. (From Mary Wollstonecraft, *A Vindication of the Rights of Woman*, ed. Carol H. Poston [New York: Norton, 1975] 191.)

If you wish to begin your sentence with the sixth word of the Wollstonecraft passage ("unless"), you must capitalize the "u" and place it in brackets to indicate your alteration of the source. But if you would rather not use square brackets to begin the sentence, then you should recast the entire sentence.

```
Mary Wollstonecraft wrote that "unless virtue be

nursed by liberty, it will never attain due

strength. . . ."
```

## 2.6.6. Punctuating quotations

The accurate quotation of sources involves a variety of punctuation, as we have already seen—parentheses for explanatory material outside a quotation, square brackets for interpolations within a quotation, and slashes between quoted lines of poetry incorporated into the text. In addition, a quotation is usually introduced by a comma or a colon. A colon precedes when a quotation is formally introduced, but either no punctuation or a comma generally precedes when the quotation serves as an integral part of the sentence.

```
Shelley argued thus: "Poets are the unacknowledged

legislators of the world."
```

but

```
Shelley thought poets "the unacknowledged

legislators of the world."
```

or

```
"Poets," according to Shelley, "are the

unacknowledged legislators of the world."
```

A quotation of verse, like a quotation set off from the text, is normally preceded by a colon.

Coleridge's <u>Rime of the Ancient Mariner</u> concludes:

"A sadder and a wiser man, / He rose the morrow

morn."

Do not use opening and closing quotation marks to enclose quotations set off from the text, but generally reproduce internal punctuation exactly as in the original. Use double quotation marks for quotations incorporated into the text, single quotation marks for quotations within those quotations.

The professor in the novel confessed that he found

it "impossible to teach Hamlet's 'To be or not to

be' speech" because he was terrified by its

implications.

Although the internal punctuation of a quotation must remain intact, the closing punctuation depends on where the quoted material appears in your sentence. Suppose, for example, that you want to quote the following sentence:

You've got to be carefully taught.

If you begin your sentence with this line, you have to replace the closing period with a punctuation mark appropriate to the new context.

"You've got to be carefully taught," wrote Oscar

Hammerstein II of racial prejudice.

Commas and periods that directly follow quotations go *inside* the closing quotation marks, but a parenthetical reference should intervene between the quotation and the required punctuation. If a quotation ends with both single and double quotation marks, the comma or period precedes both:

"Read 'Kubla Khan,'" he told me.

All other punctuation marks—such as semicolons, colons, question marks, and exclamation points—go outside quotation marks, except when they are part of the quoted material.

**Original**
I believe taxation without representation is tyranny!

**Quoted**

```
He attacked "taxation without representation"

(32).


Did he attack "taxation without representation"?


He did not even attack "taxation without

representation"!
```

but

```
He declared that "taxation without representation

is tyranny!"
```

## 2.7.  Languages other than English

The following section contains rules for expressing names of persons and for capitalizing in French, German, Italian, Spanish, and Latin. If you need such rules for other languages or if you need information on transliteration from languages using different alphabets, such as Russian or Chinese, consult *The MLA Style Manual*.

### 2.7.1.  French

#### Names of persons

With some exceptions, French *de* following a given name or a title such as *Mme* or *duc* is not used with the last name alone:

La Boétie, Etienne de
La Bruyère, Jean de
Maupassant, Guy de
Nemours, duc de
Ronsard, Pierre de
Scudéry, Madeleine de

When the last name has only one syllable, however, *de* is usually retained:

De Gaulle, Charles

The preposition also remains, in the form *d'*, when it elides with a last name beginning with a vowel:

d'Arcy, Pierre
d'Arsonval, Arsène

Similarly the forms *du* and *des*—combinations of *de* with a following *le* or *les*—are always used with the last name:

Des Périers, Bonaventure
Du Bartas, Guillaume de Salluste

A hyphen is normally used between French given names (M.-J. Chénier is Marie-Joseph Chénier, but M. R. Char is Monsieur René Char, P. J. Reynard is Père J. Reynard).

### Capitalization

In prose or verse, French usage follows English except that the following terms are not capitalized unless they begin sentences or, sometimes, lines of verse: (1) the subject pronoun *je* 'I,' (2) days and months, (3) the names of languages and the adjectives derived from proper nouns, (4) titles preceding personal names and the words for street, square, and similar places.

Un Français m'a parlé anglais place de la

Concorde.

Hier j'ai vu le docteur Maurois qui conduisait une voiture Ford.

Le capitaine Boutillier m'a dit qu'il partait pour Rouen le premier jeudi d'avril avec quelques amis normands.

In both titles and subtitles, capitalize the first words and all proper nouns.

Du côté de chez Swann

Le grand Meaulnes

La guerre de Troie n'aura pas lieu

Nouvelle revue des deux mondes

L'ami du peuple

Some instructors, however, follow other rules. When the title of a work begins with an article, they also capitalize the first noun and any preceding adjectives. In titles of series and periodicals, they capitalize all major words.

## 2.7.2.   German

### Names of persons

German *von* is generally not used with the last name alone, but there are some exceptions, especially in English contexts, where the *von* is firmly established by convention.

Droste-Hülshoff, Annette von
Kleist, Heinrich von

but

Von Braun, Wernher

Alphabetize German names with umlauts (ä, ö, ü) as they are in Germany, without regard to the umlaut. Do not, for example, convert ü to ue.

### Capitalization

In prose or verse, German usage follows English, with some important exceptions. Always capitalized in German are (1) all substantives, including any adjectives, infinitives, pronouns, prepositions, or other parts of speech used as substantives, and (2) the pronoun *Sie* 'you' and its possessive *Ihr* 'your' and their inflected forms. Not capitalized unless they begin sentences or, usually, lines of verse are (1) the subject pronoun *ich* 'I,' (2) days of the week or names of languages when used as adjectives or adverbs, and (3) adjectives and adverbs formed from proper nouns, except that those derived from personal names are always capitalized when they refer explicitly to the works and deeds of those persons.

```
Ich glaube an das Gute in der Welt.


Er schreibt, nur um dem Auf und Ab der

Buch-Nachfrage zu entsprechen.


Fahren Sie mit Ihrer Frau zurück?


Ein französischer Schriftsteller, den ich gut

kenne, arbeitet sonntags immer an seinem neuen

Buch über die platonische Liebe.


Der Staat ist eine der bekanntesten Platonischen

Schriften.
```

In letters and ceremonial writings, the pronouns *du* and *ihr* 'you' and their derivatives are capitalized.

In titles and subtitles, capitalize the first words and all words normally capitalized.

**Ein treuer Diener seines Herrn**

**Thomas Mann und die Grenzen des Ich**

**Zeitschrift für vergleichende Sprachforschung**

## 2.7.3.   Italian

### Names of persons

The names of many Italians who lived before or during the Renaissance are alphabetized by first name.

Bonvesin de la Riva
Cino da Pistoia
Dante Alighieri
Iacopone da Todi
Michelangelo Buonarroti

But other names of the period follow the standard practice.

Boccaccio, Giovanni
Cellini, Benvenuto
Stampa, Gaspara

The names of members of historic families are also usually alphabetized by the last names.

Este, Beatrice d'
Medici, Lorenzo de'

In modern times, the Italian *da*, *de*, *del*, *della*, and *di* are used with the last name. They are usually capitalized and are treated as an integral part of the name, even though a space may separate the prepositional from the nominal part of the name.

D'Annunzio, Gabriele
De Sanctis, Francesco
Del Buono, Oreste
Della Casa, Giovanni
Di Costanzo, Angelo

### Capitalization

In prose or verse, Italian usage follows English except that the following terms are not capitalized unless they begin sentences or, usually, lines of verse: (1) the subject pronoun *io* 'I,' (2) days and months, (3) names of languages, (4) nouns, adjectives, and adverbs derived from proper nouns, and (5) titles preceding personal names and the words for street, square, and similar places. But centuries and other large divisions of time are capitalized.

```
Un italiano parlava francese con uno svizzero in

piazza di Spagna.
```

```
Il dottor Bruno ritornerà dall'Italia giovedì otto

agosto e io partirò il nove.
```

```
la lirica del Novecento

il Rinascimento
```

In both titles and subtitles, capitalize only the first word and all words normally capitalized.

```
Dizionario letterario Bompiani

Bibliografia della critica pirandelliana

L'arte tipografica in Urbino

Collezione di classici italiani

Studi petrarcheschi
```

## 2.7.4.  Spanish

### Names of persons

Spanish *de* is not used before the last name alone.

Las Casas, Bartolome de
Madariaga, Salvador de
Rueda, Lope de
Timoneda, Juan de

Spanish *del*, formed from the fusion of the preposition *de* and the definite article *el*, must be used with the last name: Del Río, Angel.

Spanish surnames often include both the paternal name and the maternal name, with or without the conjunction *y*. The surname of a married woman usually includes her paternal surname and the paternal surname of the husband, connected by *de*. To index Spanish names properly, you have to distinguish between given names and surnames (your sources or a biographical dictionary can provide guidance). Alphabetize by paternal name.

Álvarez, Miguel de los Sántos
Cervantes Saavedra, Miguel de
Díaz de Castillo, Bernal
Figuera Aymerich, Ángela
Larra y Sánchez de Castro, Mariano José
López de Ayala, Pero
Matute, Ana María
Ortega y Gasset, José
Quevedo y Villegas, Francisco Gómez de
Sinues de Marco, María del Pilar
Zayas y Sotomayor, María de

Even persons commonly known by the maternal portions of their surnames—Galdós, Lorca—should be indexed under their full surnames:

García Lorca, Federico
Pérez Galdós, Benito

### Capitalization

In prose or verse, Spanish usage follows English except that the following terms are not capitalized unless they begin sentences or, sometimes, lines of verse: (1) the subject pronoun *yo* 'I,' (2) days and months, (3) nouns or adjectives derived from proper nouns, (4) titles preceding personal names and the words for street, square, and similar places.

El francés hablaba inglés en la plaza Colón.


Ayer yo vi al doctor García, que manejaba un coche

Ford.


Me dijo don Jorge que iba a salir para Sevilla el

primer martes de abril con unos amigos

neoyorkinos.

In both titles and subtitles, capitalize only the first words and words normally capitalized.

Historia verdadera de la conquista de la Nueva

　　España

La gloria de don Ramiro

Extremos de América

Trasmundo de Goya

Breve historia del ensayo hispanoamericano

Revista de filología española


## 2.7.5.　Latin

### Names of persons

Roman male citizens generally had three names: praenomen (given name), nomen (clan name), and cognomen (family or familiar name).

Men in this category are usually referred to by nomen, cognomen, or both; your source or a standard reference book such as the *Oxford Classical Dictionary* will provide guidance.

Brutus (Marcus Iunius Brutus)
Calpurnius Siculus (Titus Calpurnius Siculus)
Cicero (Marcus Tullius Cicero)
Lucretius (Titus Lucretius Carus)
Plautus (Titus Maccius Plautus)

Roman women usually had two names: nomen (the clan name in the feminine form) and cognomen (often derived from the father's cognomen): Livia Drusilla (daughter of Marcus Livius Drusus). Sometimes a woman's cognomen indicated her chronological order among the daughters of the family: Antonia Minor (younger daughter of Marcus Antonius). Most Roman women are referred to by nomen: Calpurnia, Clodia, Octavia, Sulpicia. Some, however, are better known by cognomen: Agrippina (Vipsania Agrippina).

When citing Roman names, use the forms most common in English:

Horace (Quintus Horatius Flaccus)
Julius Caesar (Gaius Iulius Caesar)
Juvenal (Decimus Iunius Iuvenalis)
Livy (Titus Livius)
Ovid (Publius Ovidius Naso)
Quintilian (Marcus Fabius Quintilianus)
Terence (Publius Terentius Afer)
Vergil (Publius Vergilius Maro)

Finally, some medieval and Renaissance figures are best known by their adopted or assigned Latin names:

Albertus Magnus (Albert von Bollstädt)
Comenius (Jan Amos Komenský)
Copernicus (Niklas Koppernigk)
Paracelsus (Theophrastus Bombast von Hohenheim)

### Capitalization

Although practice varies, Latin most commonly follows the English rules for capitalization, except that *ego* 'I' is not capitalized.

Semper ego auditor tantum? Numquamne reponam

Vexatus totiens rauci Theseide Cordi?


Quidquid id est, timeo Danaos et dona ferentes.

Nil desperandum.

Quo usque tandem abutere, Catilina, patientia

nostra?

In both titles and subtitles, however, capitalize only the first words and all words normally capitalized.

<u>De senectute</u>

<u>Liber de senectute</u>

<u>Medievalia et humanistica</u>

# 3 FORMAT OF THE RESEARCH PAPER

Your instructor may have specific requirements for the format of a research paper. Check these instructions before preparing your final draft. The following recommendations are the most common.

## 3.1. Typing

Use fresh black ribbon and clean type. Avoid typewriters with "script" or other fancy print. Type on only one side of the paper; do not use the other side for any purpose. Instructors who accept handwritten work also require neatness, legibility, dark blue or black ink, and the use of only one side of the paper. Be sure to keep a copy of the paper.

## 3.2. Paper

Use only white, twenty-pound, 8½- by 11-inch paper. Do not submit any work typed on erasable paper, which smudges easily. If you find erasable paper convenient to use, turn in a photocopy on "plain" (not coated) paper. Never use thin paper except for a carbon copy.

## 3.3. Margins

Except for page numbers, leave one-inch margins at the top and bottom and on both sides of the text. (For placement of page numbers, see 3.6.) Indent the first word of a paragraph five spaces from the left margin. Indent set-off quotations ten spaces from the left margin. (For examples, see section 2.6 and the sample first page of the research paper at the end of this book.)

## 3.4. Spacing

The research paper should be double-spaced throughout, including the heading, the title, quotations, and the bibliography. In a handwritten paper, indicate double-spacing by skipping one ruled line. (See the sample pages of a research paper at the end of this book.)

## 3.5. Heading and title of the paper

*↗ does for Davis*

A research paper does not need a title page. Instead, beginning one inch from the top of the first page and flush with the left margin, type your name, your instructor's name, the course number, and the date on separate lines, with double-spacing between the lines. Double-space again and center the title. Double-space also between lines of the title (if it has more than one line), and double-space twice between the title and the first line of the text.

*Name on first page    do same but also must have title page, also*

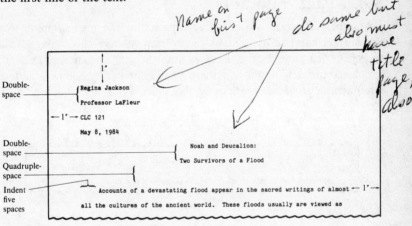

Do not underline your title or put it in quotation marks or type it in all capital letters. Follow the rules for capitalization in 2.5.1, and underline only those words that you would underline in the text (see 2.2.8).

Local Television Coverage of Recent International

  News Events

The Attitude toward Violence in Anthony Burgess's

  A Clockwork Orange

Vergil and the <u>Locus Amoenus</u> Tradition in Latin

Literature

The Use of the Noun <u>Chevisaunce</u> in Chaucer and

Spenser

Do not use a period after your title or after any heading (such as "Works Cited").

## 3.6.  Page numbers        *do not number first page*

Number *all* pages consecutively throughout the manuscript in the upper right-hand corner, one-half inch from the top. (From page 2 on, type your last name before the page number, as a precaution in case of misplaced pages.) Do not punctuate a page number by adding a period, a hyphen, or any other mark or symbol (such as the abbreviation "p.").

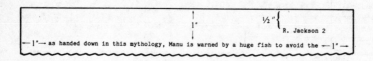

## 3.7.  Tables and illustrations

Place illustrative material as close as possible to the part of the text that it illustrates. A table is usually labeled "Table," given an arabic numeral, and captioned. Type both label and caption flush left on separate lines above the table and capitalize them as you would a title (do not use all capital letters). Give the source of the table and any notes immediately below the table. To avoid any confusion between notes to the text and notes to the table, use lowercase letters rather than numerals for notes to the table. Double-space throughout, making ruled lines as needed.

Any other type of illustrative material—for example, a photograph, map, line drawing, graph, or chart—should be labeled "Figure" (usually abbreviated "Fig."), assigned an arabic numeral, and given a title or caption: Fig. 1. Cousin, *Eva Prima Pandora*, Louvre, Paris. A label, title, or caption is ordinarily given directly below the illustration, flush with the left margin.

Table 1

Higher Education Institutions in the United States

| Type of institution | Public | Private | Total |
|---|---|---|---|
| Doctoral-granting universities | 108 | 65 | 173 |
| Comprehensive colleges and universities | 308 | 145 | 453 |
| Liberal arts colleges | 28 | 691 | 719 |
| Two-year institutions | 805 | 256 | 1,061 |
| Specialized institutions[a] | 64 | 357 | 421 |
| Total | 1,313 | 1,514 | 2,827 |

Source: ADE Bulletin 45 (1975): 1.

[a] This group consists mainly of seminaries and medical, engineering, and law schools.

Fig. 1.  Unicorn, woodcut from Edward Toppsell,

The History of Four-Footed Beasts and

Serpents . . . (London, 1658) 551; rpt. in Konrad

Gesner, Curious Woodcuts of Fanciful and Real

Beasts (New York: Dover, 1971) 27.

*Davis allows write out or ∧ + write them in in ink*

## 3.8.  Corrections and insertions

Proofread and correct your research paper carefully before submitting it. If your instructor permits brief corrections, type them (or write them neatly and legibly in ink) directly above the lines involved, using carets ( ∧ ) to indicate where they go. Do not use the margins or write below a line. If corrections on any one page are numerous or substantial, retype the page.

## 3.9.  Binding

Although a plastic folder or some other kind of binder may seem an attractive finishing touch to your research paper, most instructors find such devices a nuisance in reading and commenting on students' work. Staples and pins are similarly bothersome to take out and replace. Of course, pages may get misplaced or lost if they are left unattached or merely folded down at the upper left-hand corners. Instructors generally prefer papers secured only by paper clips, which may be easily removed and restored.

# 4  PREPARING THE LIST OF WORKS CITED

## 4.1.  General guidelines

In writing a research paper, you must indicate exactly where you found whatever material you borrow—whether facts, opinions, or quotations. This handbook recommends that you acknowledge your sources by keying citations in the text to a list of the research materials you have used. Although this list will appear at the end of your paper, you should draft it in advance, recording the works you plan to mention so that you will know what information to give in parenthetical references as you write. This chapter explains how to prepare a list of works cited, and the next chapter demonstrates how to document sources where you use them in your text. (For information concerning other systems of documentation, such as endnotes and footnotes, see 5.7–8.)

The **Works Cited** section of your paper should list all the works that have contributed ideas and information to your text. It simplifies documentation because it permits you to make only brief references to these works in the text. A citation such as "(Thompson 32–35)" enables readers to identify the source in the **Works Cited**. Other names for such a listing are **Bibliography** (literally, "description of books") and **Literature Cited**. Usually, however, the broader title **Works Cited** is more appropriate, since research papers often draw on not only books and articles but also films, recordings, television programs, and other nonprint sources.

Titles used for other kinds of source lists include **Annotated Bibliography**, **Works Consulted**, and **Selected Bibliography**. An **Annotated Bibliography**, or an **Annotated List of Works Cited**, contains descriptive or evaluative comments on the sources.

```
Thompson, Stith. The Folktale. New York: Dryden,

     1946. A comprehensive survey of the most

     popular folktales, including their histories

     and their uses in literary works.
```

The title **Works Consulted** indicates that the list is not confined to works cited in the paper. A **Selected Bibliography**, or a **Selected List of Works Consulted**, suggests readings in the field.

## 4.2.  Placement

Start the list of works cited on a new page. Number each page of the list, continuing the page numbers of the text. For example, if the text of your research paper ends on page 10, the list of works cited will begin on page 11. Type the page number in the upper right-hand corner, one-half inch from the top. Type the title **Works Cited** centered and one inch from the top of the page. Double-space between the title and the first entry. Begin the entry flush with the left margin. If an entry runs more than one line, indent the subsequent line or lines five spaces from the left margin. Double-space the entire list, between entries as well as within entries. Continue the list on as many pages as necessary.

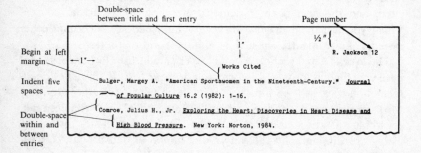

## 4.3.  Arrangement

In general, alphabetize entries in the list of works cited by the author's last name or, if the author's name is unknown, by the first word in the title other than *A*, *An*, or *The* (*An Encyclopedia of the Latin-American Novel* would be alphabetized under "E"). The alphabetical listing, as we explain at greater length in the next chapter, makes it easy for the reader to find full publication information for works referred to in the text.

Other kinds of bibliographies may be arranged differently. An annotated list, a list of works consulted, or a list of selected readings for a historical study, for example, may be organized chronologically by publication date. Some bibliographies are divided into sections, with the items alphabetized in each. A list may be broken down into primary sources and secondary sources or into different research media: books, articles, and recordings. Alternatively, it may be arranged by subject matter (e.g., Literature and Law, Law in Literature, Law as Literature), by period (e.g., Classical Utopia, Renaissance Utopia), or by area (e.g., Egyptian Mythology, Greek Mythology, Norse Mythology).

# 4.4.  Citing books: Information required

## 4.4.1.  General guidelines

An entry in a list of works cited characteristically has three main divisions—author, title, and publication information—each followed by a period and two spaces.

```
Lobdell, Jared.  England and Always: Tolkien's

    World of the Rings.  Grand Rapids: Eerdmans,

    1981.
```

Sometimes, however, other facts are required, and a period and two spaces follow each additional item of information.

```
Porter, Katherine Anne.  "Pale Horse, Pale Rider."

    Norton Anthology of World Masterpieces.  Ed.

    Maynard Mack et al.  4th ed.  2 vols.  New

    York: Norton, 1979.  2: 1606-47.
```

In citing books, normally arrange the information in the following order:

1.  Author's name
2.  Title of the part of the book
3.  Title of the book
4.  Name of the editor, translator, or compiler
5.  Edition used
6.  Number of volumes
7.  Name of the series
8.  Place of publication, name of the publisher, and date of publication
9.  Page numbers

Each of these items of information is discussed in general terms in 4.4.2–10, and examples of these recommendations are given in 4.5.

## 4.4.2.  Author's name

Reverse the author's name for alphabetizing, adding a comma after the last name: Porter, Katherine Anne. Follow the name with a period and leave two spaces before beginning the next item.

Always give the author's name as it appears on the title page. Never abbreviate a name given in full. If, for example, the title page lists the author as "Carleton Brown," do not enter the book under "Brown, C." But use initials if the title page does.

Eliot, T. S.

McLuhan, H. Marshall.

You may use square brackets to indicate a full name not found in the work cited if you think this additional information would be helpful to readers. You might supply it, for example, if you use the full name in your text or if another source uses it.

Hinton, S[usan] E[loise].

Tolkien, J[ohn] R[onald] R[euel].

Similarly, use square brackets if you wish to indicate the real name of an author listed under a pseudonym.

Le Carré, John [David Cornwell].

Svevo, Italo [Ettore Schmitz].

Occasionally, it is more appropriate to begin an entry by naming not the author but the editor or translator (see 4.5.2, 4.5.12–13). To cite an anonymous book or a book by a corporate author, see 4.5.6–7; a work written by more than one author, 4.5.4; two or more books by the same author or authors, 4.5.3–4.

## 4.4.3.  Title of part of a book

To cite only a part of a book, state the title or name of the part of the book after the author's name. To cite a work in an anthology (e.g., an essay, a short story, a poem, or a play), see 4.5.8; a book division that has only a general name, such as an introduction or a preface, 4.5.9; two or more pieces from a single book, 4.5.10.

## 4.4.4.  Title of the book

Give the full title of the book, including any subtitle. If a book has both a title and a subtitle, put a colon directly after the title, unless the title itself ends in a punctuation mark (e.g., a question mark, an exclamation mark, or a period), and skip a space before giving the subtitle. Place a period after the entire title (the title and any subtitle) unless it ends in a punctuation mark and skip two spaces before beginning the next item. Type a line under the entire title, including the colon, the subtitle, and whatever punctuation the title contains, but do not underline the period that follows the title.

Follow the recommendations for titles given in 2.5.

## 4.4.5.  Name of editor, translator, or compiler

If the name of an editor, translator, or compiler appears on the title page, it is usually appropriate to include it after the title of the work (see 4.5.12–13). To cite writers of introductions, prefaces, forewords, and afterwords, see 4.5.9.

## 4.4.6.  Edition used

A book that gives no edition number or name on its title page is probably a first edition, as your reader will assume if your bibliographic entry does not indicate otherwise. If, however, you are using a later edition of a work, identify it in your entry by number (e.g., 2nd ed., 3rd ed., or 4th ed.), by name (e.g., Rev. ed., for "revised edition"), or by year (e.g., 1984 ed.)—whichever the title page indicates. Works revised on an annual or other regular basis commonly designate successive editions by year (see 4.5.15).

## 4.4.7.  Number of volumes

In citing a multivolume work, always state the complete number of volumes (see 4.5.11).

## 4.4.8.  Series

In citing a book that is part of a publication series, give the name of the series and the arabic numeral denoting the work's place in the series (see 4.5.18).

## 4.4.9.  Place of publication, publisher, and date of publication

Give the city of publication, the publisher's name, and the year of publication (for a few exceptions, see 4.5.15 and 4.5.24–25). Take these facts directly from the book itself, not from a source such as a bibliography or a library catalog. Publication information usually appears on the title page, the copyright page (i.e., the reverse of the title page), or, particularly in books published outside the United States, the colophon at the back of the book. Use a colon and a space between the place of publication and the publisher, a comma and a space between the publisher and the date, and a period after the date.

Since the city of publication is sometimes needed to identify a book, it should always be given. If several cities are listed for the publisher, give only the first. For cities outside the United States, add an abbreviation of the country (or province for cities in Canada) if the name of the city may be ambiguous or unfamiliar to your reader: Manchester, Eng.; Sherbrooke, Qué. (see 6.3 for abbreviations of geographical names). To cite the city of publication for a book published in a language other than English, see 4.5.22. If no place of publication is given, write "N.p." for "no place" (see 4.5.25).

Use an appropriately shortened form of the publisher's name, following the guidelines in 6.5. To cite a work issued under a publisher's special imprint, give the imprint and add the publisher's name after a hyphen: Del Rey-Ballantine (see 4.5.19). If the title page indicates that two publishers have brought out the work simultaneously, give both (see 4.5.20). You may omit the name of a publisher for a work published before 1900 (see 4.5.24). If no publisher is given for a later work, write "n.p." for "no publisher" after the colon (see 4.5.25); if a work is privately printed, write "privately printed" (see 4.5.27).

After the publisher's name, a comma, and a space, write the year in which the book was published. If this date is not recorded on the title or copyright page or in the colophon, use the latest copyright date. If the copyright page indicates that the work has had several printings (or "impressions") by the same publisher, use the original publication date. But in citing a new or revised edition, give the date of that edition, not the original date. If you are listing a reprint by a different publisher— for instance, a paperback reprint of a book originally published in a clothbound edition—give the dates of both the original edition and the reprint (see 4.5.14). In citing a multivolume work published over a number of years, give the inclusive dates (see 4.5.11). If no date of publication is printed in the book, write "n.d." (see 4.5.25) or supply in square brackets an approximate date and a question mark. If the date is known, though missing in the book, omit the question mark.

## 4.4.10.   Page numbers

Give the inclusive page numbers when you cite part of a book (e.g., an essay, short story, or preface). Be sure to give the page numbers of the *entire* piece, not just the pages for the material you have used; specific page references will appear, in parentheses, within the text (see ch.

5). Inclusive page numbers, usually without any identifying abbreviation, follow the publication date, a period, and two spaces (see 4.5.8). For a multivolume work, the page numbers should follow the volume number, a colon, and a space (see 4.5.11). If the book has no pagination, you may indicate "N. pag." as part of the entry (see 4.5.25).

## 4.5. Sample entries: Books

The following examples illustrate the recommendations in 4.4.

### 4.5.1. A book by a single author

To cite a book by a single author, follow the general pattern outlined in 4.4: author's name (reversed for alphabetizing), title (including any subtitle), and publication information (city of publication, publisher, date of publication).

Clark, Kenneth. <u>What Is a Masterpiece?</u> London:

    Thames, 1979.

Hinton, S[usan] E[loise]. <u>The Outsiders</u>. New

    York: Viking, 1967.

Le Carré, John [David Cornwell]. <u>Tinker, Tailor,</u>

    <u>Soldier, Spy</u>. New York: Knopf, 1974.

McConnell, Frank. <u>Storytelling and Mythmaking:</u>

    <u>Images from Film and Literature</u>. New York:

    Oxford UP, 1979.

### 4.5.2. An anthology or a compilation

To cite an anthology or a compilation (e.g., a bibliography), record first the name of the editor or compiler, followed by a comma, a space, and the abbreviation "ed." or "comp." If the person has performed more than one function—serving, say, as editor and translator—give both roles.

Gunn, Giles, ed. <u>Literature and Religion</u>. New

    York: Harper, 1971.

Nichols, Fred J., ed. and trans. <u>An Anthology of</u>

><u>Neo-Latin Poetry</u>. New Haven: Yale UP, 1979.

Stratman, Carl J., comp. and ed. <u>Bibliography of</u>

><u>English Printed Tragedy, 1565-1900</u>.

>Carbondale: Southern Illinois UP, 1966.

See also the sections on works in an anthology (4.5.8), introductions and prefaces to books (4.5.9), editions (4.5.12), and translations (4.5.13).

## 4.5.3. Two or more books by the same person

In citing two or more books by the same person, give the name in the first entry only. Thereafter, in place of the name, type three hyphens and a period, skip two spaces, and give the title. The three hyphens always stand for exactly the same name(s) as in the preceding entry. If the person named served as editor, translator, or compiler of any of the books, place a comma (not a period) after the three hyphens, skip a space, and write the appropriate abbreviation (ed., trans., or comp.) before giving the title. If the same person served as, say, the editor of two or more works listed consecutively, the abbreviation "ed." must be repeated with each entry. This sort of label, however, does not affect the order in which entries appear; works listed under the same name(s) are alphabetized by title.

Borroff, Marie. <u>Language and the Past: Verbal</u>

><u>Artistry in Frost, Stevens, and Moore</u>.

>Chicago: U of Chicago P, 1979.

---, trans. <u>Sir Gawain and the Green Knight</u>. New

>York: Norton, 1967.

---, ed. <u>Wallace Stevens: A Collection of</u>

><u>Critical Essays</u>. Englewood Cliffs: Prentice,

>1963.

```
Frye, Northrop.  Anatomy of Criticism: Four

     Essays.  Princeton: Princeton UP, 1957.

---, ed.  Sound and Poetry.  New York: Columbia

     UP, 1957.

---.  A Study of English Romanticism.  New York:

     Random, 1968.
```

## 4.5.4. A book by two or more persons

In citing a book by two or more persons, give their names in the order in which they appear on the title page—not necessarily in alphabetical order. Reverse only the name of the first author, add a comma, and give the other name(s) in normal order: Wellek, René, and Austin Warren. Place a period after the last name, skip two spaces, and begin the next item. Even if the authors have the same last name, state each name in full: Durant, Will, and Ariel Durant. If there are more than three authors, name only the first and add "et al." ("and others"). If the persons listed on the title page are editors, translators, or compilers, place a comma (not a period) after the last name and add the appropriate abbreviation (eds., trans., or comps.).

```
Blocker, Clyde E., Robert H. Plummer, and Richard

     C. Richardson, Jr.  The Two-Year College: A

     Social Synthesis.  Englewood Cliffs:

     Prentice, 1965.

Bondanella, Peter, and Julia Conaway Bondanella,

     eds.  Dictionary of Italian Literature.

     Westport: Greenwood, 1979.

Edens, Walter, et al., eds.  Teaching

     Shakespeare.  Princeton: Princeton UP, 1977.
```

Scholes, Robert, and Eric Rabkin. <u>Science</u>

    <u>Fiction: History, Science, Vision</u>. New York:

    Oxford UP, 1977.

If a single author cited in an entry is also the first of multiple authors in the following entry, repeat the name in full; do not substitute three hyphens. Likewise, repeat the name in full whenever you cite the same person as part of a different authorship. Remember that the three hyphens always stand for exactly the same name(s) as in the preceding entry.

Knoepflmacher, U. C. <u>Religious Humanism and the</u>

    <u>Victorian Novel: George Eliot, Walter Pater,</u>

    <u>and Samuel Butler</u>. Princeton: Princeton UP,

    1970.

Knoepflmacher, U. C., and G. B. Tennyson, eds.

    <u>Nature and the Victorian Imagination</u>.

    Berkeley: U of California P, 1977.

Tennyson, G. B., ed. <u>An Introduction to Drama</u>.

    New York: Holt, 1967.

---. <u>Victorian Devotional Poetry: The Tractarian</u>

    <u>Mode</u>. Cambridge: Harvard UP, 1981.

Tennyson, G. B., and Edward Ericson, Jr., eds.

    <u>Religion and Modern Literature: Essays in</u>

    <u>Theory and Criticism</u>. Grand Rapids:

    Eerdmans, 1975.

Tennyson, G. B., and Donald Gray, eds. <u>Victorian</u>

    <u>Literature: Prose</u>. New York: Macmillan,

    1976.

## 4.5.5. Two or more books by the same multiple authors

In citing two or more works by the same multiple authors, give the names of the authors in the first entry only. Thereafter, in place of the names, type three hyphens, followed with a period; skip two spaces, and give the next title. The three hyphens always stand for exactly the same name(s) as in the preceding entry.

Durant, Will. <u>The Age of Faith</u>. Vol. 4 of <u>The</u>

    <u>Story of Civilization</u>. New York: Simon,

    1950.

---. <u>Our Oriental Heritage</u>. Vol. 1 of <u>The Story</u>

    <u>of Civilization</u>. New York: Simon, 1935.

Durant, Will, and Ariel Durant. <u>The Age of</u>

    <u>Voltaire</u>. Vol. 9 of <u>The Story of</u>

    <u>Civilization</u>. New York: Simon, 1965.

---. <u>A Dual Autobiography</u>. New York: Simon,

    1977.

---. <u>Rousseau and Romanticism</u>. Vol. 10 of <u>The</u>

    <u>Story of Civilization</u>. New York: Simon,

    1967.

## 4.5.6. A book by a corporate author

Cite the book by the corporate author, even if the corporate author is the publisher. (On citing government publications, see 4.5.17.)

American Council on Education. <u>Annual Report,</u>

<u>1970</u>. Washington: American Council on Educ.,

1971.

Carnegie Council on Policy Studies in Higher

Education. <u>Giving Youth a Better Chance:</u>

<u>Options for Education, Work, and Service</u>.

San Francisco: Jossey, 1980.

Commission on the Humanities. <u>The Humanities in</u>

<u>American Life: Report of the Commission on</u>

<u>the Humanities</u>. Berkeley: U of California P,

1980.

National Committee on Careers for Older Americans.

<u>Older Americans: An Untapped Resource</u>.

Washington: Acad. for Educ. Dev., 1979.


## 4.5.7.  An anonymous book

If a book has no author's name on the title page, do not use either
"Anonymous" or "Anon." Begin the entry with the title and alphabetize by the first word other than a definite or indefinite article. (In the
sample entries, note that *A Handbook of Korea* is alphabetized under
"H.")

<u>Dictionary of Ancient Greek Civilization</u>. London:

Methuen, 1966.

A Handbook of Korea. 4th ed. Seoul: Korean

Overseas Information Service, Ministry of

Culture and Information, 1982.

Literary Market Place: The Directory of American

Book Publishing. 1984 ed. New York: Bowker,

1983.

The Times Atlas of the World. 5th ed. New York:

New York Times, 1975.

## 4.5.8.  A work in an anthology

First, state the author and title of the piece you are citing (e.g., an essay, a short story, or a poem), normally enclosing the title in quotation marks but underlining instead if the work was originally published as a book (e.g., a play or a novel; see sample entries for "Hansberry" and "Unamuno y Jugo"). If the anthology contains works by different translators, give the translator's name next, preceded by the abbreviation "Trans." (see entry for "Unamuno y Jugo") and followed by the title of the anthology (underlined). If all the works have the same translator or if the collection has an editor, write "Trans." or "Ed." (or "Ed. and trans.") after the title and give that person's name. Cite the inclusive pages for the piece at the end of the citation, after the year of publication, a period, and two spaces.

Auerbach, Erich.  "Odysseus' Scar."  Mimesis: The

Representation of Reality in Western

Literature.  Trans. Willard R. Trask.

Princeton: Princeton UP, 1953.  3-23.

García Márquez, Gabriel.  "A Very Old Man with

Enormous Wings."  "Leaf Storm" and Other

Stories. Trans. Gregory Rabassa. New York:

Harper, 1972. 105-12.

Hansberry, Lorraine. A Raisin in the Sun. Black

Theater: A Twentieth-Century Collection of

the Work of Its Best Playwrights. Ed.

Lindsay Patterson. New York: Dodd, 1971.

221-76.

O'Connor, Flannery. "The Life You Save May Be

Your Own." The Realm of Fiction:

Seventy-Four Stories. Ed. James B. Hall and

Elizabeth C. Hall. 3rd ed. New York:

McGraw, 1977. 479-88.

Unamuno y Jugo, Miguel de. Abel Sanchez. Trans.

Anthony Kerrigan. Eleven Modern Short

Novels. Ed. Leo Hamalian and Edmond L.

Volpe. 2nd ed. New York: Putnam's, 1970.

253-350.

In citing an article or essay in a collection of previously published works, give the complete data for the earlier publication and then add "Rpt. in" ("Reprinted in"), the title of the collection, and the new publication facts.

Hamilton, Marie Padgett. "The Meaning of the

Middle English Pearl." PMLA 20 (1955):

805-24. Rpt. in <u>Middle English Survey:</u>

<u>Critical Essays</u>. Ed. Edward Vasta. Notre

Dame: U of Notre Dame P, 1965. 117-45.

If a new title has been assigned to the piece, give the original title as well as the original publication information, followed by "Rpt. as" ("Reprinted as") and the new title and publication facts.

Lewis, C. S. "The Anthropological Approach."

<u>English and Medieval Studies Presented to</u>

<u>J. R. R. Tolkien on the Occasion of His</u>

<u>Seventieth Birthday</u>. Ed. Norman Davis and C.

L. Wrenn. London: Allen, 1962. 219-23.

Rpt. as "Viewpoints: C. S. Lewis." <u>Twentieth</u>

<u>Century Interpretations of</u> Sir Gawain and the

Green Knight. Ed. Denton Fox. Englewood

Cliffs: Prentice, 1968. 100-01.

If you refer to more than one piece from the same collection, you may wish to cross-reference each citation to a single entry for the book itself (see 4.5.10). On citing introductions and prefaces, see 4.5.9. On citing a piece in a multivolume anthology, see 4.5.11.

## 4.5.9. An introduction, preface, foreword, or afterword

To cite an introduction, preface, foreword, or afterword, begin with the name of its author and then give the name of the part being cited, capitalized but neither underlined nor put in quotation marks (Introduction, Preface, Foreword, Afterword). If the writer of the piece is different from the author of the complete work, cite the author of the work after the title, giving the full name, in normal order, preceded by the word "By." If the writer of the piece is also the author of the complete work, use only the last name after "By."

Borges, Jorge Luis.  Foreword.  <u>Selected Poems,</u>

　　<u>1923-1967</u>.  By Borges.  Ed. Norman Thomas Di

　　Giovanni.  New York: Delta-Dell, 1973.

　　xv-xvi.

Doctorow, E. L.  Introduction.  <u>Sister Carrie</u>.  By

　　Theodore Dreiser.  New York: Bantam, 1982.

　　v-xi.

Johnson, Edgar.  Afterword.  <u>David Copperfield</u>.

　　By Charles Dickens.  New York: Signet-NAL,

　　1962.  871-79.

## 4.5.10.  Cross-references

If you are citing two or more works from the same collection, you may, to avoid unnecessary repetition, list the collection itself, with complete publication information, and cite individual pieces by using cross-references to the main entry. In a cross-reference, the last name of the editor of the collection and the relevant page numbers follow the author's name and the title of the piece.

Chesebro, James W.  "Communication, Values, and

　　Popular Television Series--A Four-Year

　　Assessment."  Newcomb 16-54.

De Lauretis, Teresa.  "A Semiotic Approach to

　　Television as Ideological Apparatus."

　　Newcomb 107-17.

Newcomb, Horace, ed. <u>Television: The Critical</u>

   <u>View</u>. 2nd ed. New York: Oxford UP, 1979.

If you list two or more works under the editor's name, however, add the title (or a shortened version of it) to the cross-reference.

Altieri, Charles. "A Procedural Definition of

   Literature." Hernadi, <u>What Is Literature?</u>

   62-78.

Beardsley, Monroe C. "The Name and Nature of

   Criticism." Hernadi, <u>What Is Criticism?</u>

   151-61.

Booth, Wayne C. "Criticulture: Or, Why We Need at

   Least Three Criticisms at the Present Time."

   Hernadi, <u>What Is Criticism?</u>  162-76.

Hernadi, Paul, ed. <u>What Is Criticism?</u>

   Bloomington: Indiana UP, 1981.

---, ed. <u>What Is Literature?</u>  Bloomington:

   Indiana UP, 1978.

Hirsch, E. D., Jr. "What Isn't Literature?"

   Hernadi, <u>What Is Literature?</u>  24-34.

## 4.5.11.  A multivolume work

   In citing a work of two or more volumes, give the total number regardless of the number you use. Add this information (e.g., 5 vols.) between the title and the publication information; specific references to volume and page numbers (e.g., 3: 212–13) belong in the text. (See ch. 5 for parenthetical documentation.)

If the volumes of the work were published over a period of years, give the inclusive dates at the end of the citation (e.g., 1952–70). If the work is still in progress, write "to date" after the number of volumes (e.g., 3 vols. to date) and leave a space after the hyphen that follows the beginning date (e.g., 1982–   ).

When citing a piece in a multivolume anthology, give the volume number and the inclusive page number(s), separated by a colon (e.g., 2: 25–32), after the publication information (see sample entry for "Arnold").

If you use only one volume of a multivolume work, include the volume number in the bibliographic entry; then you need give only page numbers when you cite that work in the text (see sample entry for "Daiches"). If the volume has an individual title, give that title after the author's name and add a period. Next cite the volume number, preceded by the abbreviation "Vol." and followed by the word "of" and the title of the complete work (see sample entry for "Churchill").

Arnold, Matthew.  "Dover Beach."  Norton Anthology

    of English Literature.  Ed. M. H. Abrams et

    al.  4th ed.  2 vols.  New York: Norton,

    1979.  2: 1378-79.

Cassirer, Ernst.  The Philosophy of Symbolic

    Forms.  Trans. Ralph Manheim.  3 vols.  New

    Haven: Yale UP, 1955.

Churchill, Winston S.  The Age of Revolution.

    Vol. 3 of A History of the English-Speaking

    Peoples.  4 vols.  New York: Dodd, 1957.

Daiches, David.  A Critical History of English

    Literature.  2nd ed.  2 vols.  New York:

Ronald, 1970.  Vol. 2.

Potter, G. R., et al.  <u>The New Cambridge Modern</u>

  <u>History</u>.  14 vols.  Cambridge: Cambridge UP,

  1957-70.

Schlesinger, Arthur M., gen. ed.  <u>History of U.S.</u>

  <u>Political Parties</u>.  4 vols.  New York:

  Chelsea, 1973.

Wing, Donald, et al., eds.  <u>Short-Title Catalogue</u>

  <u>of Books Printed in England, Scotland,</u>

  <u>Ireland, Wales, and British America and of</u>

  <u>English Books Printed in Other Countries,</u>

  <u>1641-1700</u>.  2nd ed.  2 vols. to date.  New

  York: MLA, 1972- .

## 4.5.12.  An "edition"

Every published book is, in one sense, an "edition"; for example, a book may be a "first edition" or a "second edition," and so forth. Researchers also use the term "edition," however, to denote a work by one person that has been prepared for printing by another, the editor. For example, a 1984 printing of Shakespeare's *Hamlet* was, obviously, not prepared for printing by Shakespeare. An editor selected a version of *Hamlet* from among the various versions available, decided on any changes in spelling or punctuation, and perhaps added explanatory notes or wrote an introduction. This 1984 version of *Hamlet* would be called an "edition" and usually the name of the editor would be stated on the title page.

To cite an edition, begin with the author if you refer primarily to the text itself; give the editor's name, preceded by the abbreviation "Ed.," after the title. If the book is a volume of a multivolume work edited by the same person, state the editor's name after the title of the multivolume work (see entry for "Arnold").

Arnold, Matthew.  <u>The Last Word</u>.  Vol. 11 of

    <u>Complete Prose Works of Matthew Arnold</u>.  Ed.

    R. H. Super.  11 vols.  Ann Arbor: U of

    Michigan P, 1960-77.

Chaucer, Geoffrey.  <u>The Works of Geoffrey</u>

    <u>Chaucer</u>.  Ed. F. N. Robinson.  2nd ed.

    Boston: Houghton, 1957.

If you cite more than one volume of a multivolume work, give one listing for the entire work. Parenthetical references in the text will document the specific volumes you use (see ch. 5).

Dewey, John.  <u>The Early Works, 1882-1898</u>.  Ed.

    Jo Ann Boydston.  4 vols.  Carbondale:

    Southern Illinois UP, 1967-71.

If the citations in your paper are to the work of the editor (e.g., the introduction or notes or the editor's decisions in editing the text), begin the entry with the editor's name followed by a comma and the abbreviation "ed.," and give the author's name, preceded by the word "By," after the title.

Bowers, Fredson, ed.  <u>The Red Badge of Courage: An</u>

    <u>Episode of the American Civil War</u>.  By

    Stephen Crane.  Vol. 2 of <u>The Works of</u>

    <u>Stephen Crane</u>.  10 vols.  Charlottesville: UP

    of Virginia, 1969-75.

## 4.5.13.  A translation

In citing a translation, state the author's name first if most of the references in your paper are to the work itself and give the translator's name, preceded by "Trans.," after the title.

Dostoevsky, Feodor. <u>Crime and Punishment</u>. Trans.

    Jessie Coulson. Ed. George Gibian. New

    York: Norton, 1964.

Metastasio, Pietro. <u>Three Melodramas</u>. Trans.

    Joseph G. Fucilla. Studies in Romance Langs.

    24. Lexington: UP of Kentucky, 1981.

Sastre, Alfonso. <u>Sad Are the Eyes of William</u>

    <u>Tell</u>. Trans. Leonard Pronko. <u>The New Wave</u>

    <u>Spanish Drama</u>. Ed. George E. Wellwarth. New

    York: New York UP, 1970. 265-321.

If the citations in your paper are to the comments of the translator, or to the translator's decisions in preparing the text, begin the bibliographic entry with the translator's name, followed by a comma and the abbreviation "trans.," and give the author's name, preceded by the word "By," after the title. (On citing anthologies of translated works by different authors, see 4.5.8.)

Coulson, Jessie, trans. <u>Crime and Punishment</u>. By

    Feodor Dostoevsky. Ed. George Gibian. New

    York: Norton, 1964.

Fucilla, Joseph G., trans. <u>Three Melodramas</u>. By

Pietro Metastasio.   Studies in Romance Langs.

24.   Lexington: UP of Kentucky, 1981.

## 4.5.14.  A republished book

In citing a republished book—for example, a paperback version of a book originally published in a clothbound version—give the date of the original edition, followed by a period and two spaces, before the publication information for the book you are citing.

Doctorow, E. L.  <u>Welcome to Hard Times</u>.   1960.

New York: Bantam, 1976.

Malamud, Bernard.  <u>The Natural</u>.  1952.  New York:

Avon, 1980.

Mead, Margaret.  <u>Blackberry Winter: My Earlier</u>

<u>Years</u>.  1972.  New York: Pocket, 1975.

## 4.5.15.  An article in a reference book

Treat an encyclopedia article or a dictionary entry as you would a piece in a collection (4.5.8), but do not cite the editor of the reference work. If the article is signed, give the author first (often articles in reference books are signed with initials identified elsewhere in the work); if it is unsigned, give the title first. If the encyclopedia or dictionary arranges articles alphabetically, you may omit volume and page numbers.

When citing familiar reference books, especially those that frequently appear in new editions, do not give full publication information. For such works, list only the edition (if stated) and the year of publication.

"Azimuthal Equidistant Projection."  <u>Webster's New</u>

<u>Collegiate Dictionary</u>.  1980 ed.

Chiappini, Luciano.  "Este, House of."

<u>Encyclopaedia Britannica: Macropaedia</u>.  1974

ed.

"Graham, Martha." Who's Who of American Women.

    13th ed. 1983-84.

"Mandarin." Encyclopedia Americana. 1980 ed.

When citing less familiar reference books, however, especially those that have appeared in only one edition, give full publication information.

Brakeley, Theresa C. "Mourning Songs." Funk and

    Wagnalls Standard Dictionary of Folklore,

    Mythology, and Legend. Ed. Maria Leach and

    Jerome Fried. 2 vols. New York: Crowell,

    1950.

Trainen, Isaac N., et al. "Religious Directives

    in Medical Ethics." Encyclopedia of

    Bioethics. Ed. Warren T. Reich. 4 vols.

    New York: Free, 1978.

## 4.5.16. A pamphlet

Treat a pamphlet as you would a book.

Capital Punishment: Cruel and Unusual? Plano:

    Instructional Aides, 1982.

Kilgus, Robert. Color Scripsit Program Manual.

    Fort Worth: Tandy, 1981.

## 4.5.17. Government publications

Because government publications emanate from many sources, they present special problems in bibliographic citation. In general, if the writer of the document is not known, treat the government agency as the author—that is, state the name of the government first, followed by the name of the agency, using an abbreviation if the context makes it clear. (But see below for citing a document whose author is known.) If you are citing two or more works issued by the same government, substitute three hyphens for the name in each entry after the first. If you cite more than one work by the same government agency, each subsequent entry should show three hyphens in place of the government and three additional hyphens in place of the agency.

`California.  Dept. of Industrial Relations.`

`United States.  Cong.  House.`

`---.  ---.  Senate.`

`---.  Dept. of Health and Human Services.`

The title of the publication, underlined, should follow immediately. In citing a congressional document other than the *Congressional Record* (which requires only a date and a page number), include such information as the number and session of Congress, the house (S or HR), and the type and number of the publication. Types of congressional publications include bills (S 33; HR 77), resolutions (S. Res. 20; H. Res. 50), reports (S. Rept. 9; H. Rept. 142), and documents (S. Doc. 333; H. Doc. 222).

The usual publishing information comes next (i.e., place, publisher, and date). Most federal publications, regardless of the branch of government, are published by the Government Printing Office (GPO) in Washington, DC; its British counterpart is Her (or His) Majesty's Stationery Office (HMSO) in London. Documents issued by the United Nations and most local governments, however, do not emanate from a central office; give the publishing information that appears on the title page.

`Cong. Rec. 7 Feb. 1973: 3831-51.`

`Great Britain.  Ministry of Defence.  Author and`

  `Subject Catalogues of the Naval Library,`

  `Ministry of Defence.  5 vols.  London: HMSO,`

  `1967.`

New York State.  Committee on State Prisons.

Investigation of the New York State Prisons.

1883.  New York: Arno, 1974.

United Nations.  Centre for National Resources.

State Petroleum Enterprises in Developing

Countries.  Elmsford: Pergamon, 1980.

---.  Economic Commission for Africa.  Industrial

Growth in Africa.  New York: United Nations,

1963.

United States.  Cong.  Joint Committee on the

Investigation of the Pearl Harbor Attack.

Hearings.  79th Cong., 1st and 2nd sess.  32

vols.  Washington: GPO, 1946.

---.  ---.  Senate.  Subcommittee on

Constitutional Amendments of the Committee on

the Judiciary.  Hearings on the "Equal

Rights" Amendment.  91st Cong., 2nd sess.  S.

Res. 61.  Washington: GPO, 1970.

---.  Dept. of Labor.  Bureau of Statistics.

Dictionary of Occupational Titles.  4th ed.

Washington: GPO, 1977.

```
---. Dept. of State.  Office of Public Affairs.

    Korea, 1945-1947: A Report on Political

    Development and Economic Resources.  1948.

    Westport: Greenwood, 1968.
```

If known, the name of the author of a government document may be given first in the entry or, if the agency is listed first, placed after the title and preceded by the word "By."

```
Washburne, E. B.  Memphis Riots and Massacres.

    U.S. 39th Cong., 2nd sess.  H. Rept. 101.

    1866.  New York: Arno, 1969.
```

or

```
United States.  Cong.  House.  Memphis Riots and

    Massacres.  By E. B. Washburne.  39th Cong.,

    2nd sess.  H. Rept. 101.  1866.  New York:

    Arno, 1969.
```

## 4.5.18.  A book in a series

If the title page or the preceding page (the half-title page) indicates that the book you are citing is part of a series, include the series name, neither underlined nor enclosed in quotation marks, and the series number, followed by a period, before the publishing information.

```
Bjornson, Richard, ed.  Approaches to Teaching

    Cervantes' Don Quixote.  Approaches to

    Teaching Masterpieces of World Literature 3.

    New York: MLA, 1984.

Curtius, Ernst Robert.  European Literature and
```

the Latin Middle Ages. Trans. Willard

Trask. Bollingen Series 36. Princeton:

Princeton UP, 1953.

Hinchcliffe, Arnold P. Harold Pinter. Rev. ed.

Twayne's English Authors Series 51. Boston:

Twayne, 1981.

## 4.5.19.  A publisher's imprint

If the title page or copyright page includes the name of a publisher's special imprint, give the publisher's name after the imprint name and a hyphen (e.g., Ace-Berkeley, Anchor-Doubleday, Belknap-Harvard UP, Camelot-Avon, Del Rey-Ballantine, Laurel Leaf-Dell, Mentor-NAL). The name of a publisher's imprint often appears above the publisher's name on the title page.

Brooks, Terry. The Elfstones of Shannara. New

York: Del Rey-Ballantine, 1982.

Hsu, Kai-yu, ed. and trans. Twentieth-Century

Chinese Poetry. Garden City:

Anchor-Doubleday, 1964.

## 4.5.20.  Multiple publishers

If the title page lists two or more publishers—not just two or more offices of the same publisher—include both, in the order given, as part of the publication information, putting a semicolon after the name of the first publisher.

Duff, J. Wight. A Literary History of Rome: From

the Origins to the Close of the Golden Age.

Ed. A. M. Duff. 3rd ed. 1953. London:

Benn; New York: Barnes, 1967.

Shelley, Percy Bysshe. <u>Selected Poems</u>. Ed.

Timothy Webb. London: Dent; Totowa: Rowman,

1977.

## 4.5.21. Published proceedings of a conference

Treat the published proceedings of a conference as you would a book, but add pertinent information about the conference (unless the book title includes such information).

Gordon, Alan M., and Evelyn Rugg, eds. <u>Actas del</u>

<u>Sexto Congreso Internacional de Hispanistas</u>

<u>celebrado en Toronto del 22 al 26 agosto de</u>

<u>1977</u>. Toronto: Dept. of Spanish and

Portuguese, U of Toronto, 1980.

<u>Humanistic Scholarship in America</u>. Proc. of a

Conference on the Princeton Studies in the

Humanities. 5-6 Nov. 1965. Princeton:

Princeton U, 1966.

When citing a particular presentation in the proceedings, treat it as a work in a collection of pieces by different authors (see 4.5.8).

## 4.5.22. A book in a language other than English

In citing a book published in a language other than English, give all information exactly as it appears on the title or copyright page or in the colophon. Provide translations, in brackets, of the title and the city of publication if clarifications seem necessary (e.g., *Et Dukkehjem* [*A Doll House*]; Wien [Vienna]). Or you may substitute the English name of a foreign city. Use appropriate abbreviations for publishers' names (see 6.5). (For capitalization in languages other than English, see 2.7.)

Dahlhaus, Carl. <u>Musikästhetik</u>. Köln: Gerig,

   1967.

Gramsci, Antonio. <u>Gli intelletuali e

   l'organizzazione della cultura</u>. Torino:

   Einaudi, 1949.

Rey-Flaud, Henri. <u>Pour une dramaturgie du Moyen

   Age</u>. Paris: PUF, 1980.

Wachowicz, Barbara. <u>Marie jeho života</u>. Praha

   [Prague]: Lidové, 1979.

## 4.5.23. A book with a title within its title

   If the book title you are citing contains a title normally enclosed within quotation marks (e.g., a short story or a poem), retain the quotation marks and underline the entire title. If the closing quotation mark appears at the end of the title, place a period before the quotation mark. If the book title you are citing contains a title normally underlined (e.g., a novel or a play), the shorter title is neither placed in quotation marks nor underlined; it appears, instead, in "roman type"—that is, not underlined.

Danzig, Allan, ed. <u>Twentieth Century

   Interpretations of "The Eve of St. Agnes."</u>

   Englewood Cliffs: Prentice, 1971.

Dunn, Richard J. David Copperfield<u>: An Annotated

   Bibliography</u>. New York: Garland, 1981.

Mades, Leonard. <u>The Armor and the Brocade: A

   Study of</u> Don Quijote <u>and</u> The Courtier. New

   York: Las Americas, 1968.

## 4.5.24. A book published before 1900

When citing a book published before 1900, you may omit the name of the publisher.

Dewey, John. <u>The Study of Ethics: A Syllabus</u>.

    Ann Arbor, 1894.

Udall, John. <u>The Combate between Christ and the</u>

    <u>Devil: Four Sermones on the Temptations of</u>

    <u>Christ</u>. London, 1589.

## 4.5.25. A book without stated publication information or pagination

When a book does not indicate the publisher, the place or date of publication, or the pagination, supply as much of the missing data as you can, enclosing such information in brackets to show that it did not come from the source:

New York: U of Gotham P, [1983].

If the date can only be approximated, put it after a "c." (for "circa" 'around'; e.g., [c. 1983]). If you are uncertain about the accuracy of the information you are supplying, add a question mark (e.g., [1983?]). If you cannot supply any information, use the following abbreviations:

n.p.        no place of publication given
n.p.        no publisher given
n.d.        no date of publication given
n. pag.      no pagination given

Inserted before the colon, the abbreviation "n.p." indicates "no place"; after the colon it indicates "no publisher." "N. pag." informs your reader why no page references for the work are included in your citations.

**No date**
New York: U of Gotham P, n.d.

**No pagination**
New York: U of Gotham P, 1983. N. pag.

 No place
N.p.: U of Gotham P, 1983.

 No publisher
New York: n.p., 1983.

 Neither place nor publisher
N.p.: n.p., 1983.

Malachi, Zvi, ed. <u>Proceedings of the</u>

 <u>International Conference on Literary and</u>

 <u>Linguistic Computing</u>. [Tel Aviv]: [Tel Aviv

 U Fac. of Humanities], n.d.

<u>Photographic View Album of Cambridge</u>. [England]:

 n.p., n.d. N. pag.

## 4.5.26. An unpublished dissertation

In citing the unpublished version of a dissertation, place the title in quotation marks; do not underline it. Then write the descriptive label "Diss.," preceded and followed by two spaces, and add the name of the degree-granting university, followed by a comma, a space, and the year.

Boyle, Anthony T. "The Epistemological Evolution

 of Renaissance Utopian Literature:

 1516-1657." Diss. New York U, 1983.

Johnson, Nancy Kay. "Cultural and Psychosocial

 Determinants of Health and Illness." Diss.

 U of Washington, 1980.

For citing a dissertation abstract published in *Dissertation Abstracts* or *Dissertation Abstracts International*, see 4.7.12. For documenting other unpublished writing, see 4.8.15.

## 4.5.27.  A published dissertation

Treat a published dissertation as you would a book, but add pertinent dissertation information and, if the work has been published by University Microfilms International (UMI), the order number.

Brewda, Lee Aaron.  <u>A Semantically-Based Verb</u>

<u>Valence Analysis of Old Saxon</u>.  Diss.

Princeton U, 1981.  Ann Arbor: UMI, 1982.

8203236.

Dietze, Rudolf F.  <u>Ralph Ellison: The Genesis of</u>

<u>an Artist</u>.  Diss.  U Erlangen-Nürnberg,

1982.  Erlanger Beiträge zur Sprach- und

Kunstwissenschaft 70.  Nürnberg: Carl, 1982.

Wendriner, Karl Georg.  <u>Der Einfluss von Goethes</u>

Wilhelm Meister <u>auf das Drama der</u>

<u>Romantiker</u>.  Diss.  U Bonn, 1907.  Leipzig:

privately printed, 1907.

# 4.6.  Citing articles in periodicals: Information required

## 4.6.1.  General guidelines

An entry for an article in a periodical, like an entry for a book, has three main divisions: author, title of the article, and publication information. For scholarly journals, publication information generally includes the journal title, volume number, the year of publication, and inclusive page numbers.

Booth, Wayne C.  "Kenneth Burke's Way of

Knowing." <u>Critical Inquiry</u> 1 (1974): 1-22.

Sometimes, however, additional information is required. In citing articles in periodicals, normally arrange the information in the following order:

1. Author's name
2. Title of the article
3. Name of the periodical
4. Series number or name
5. Volume number
6. Date of publication
7. Page numbers

Each of these items of information is discussed in general terms in 4.6.2–8, and examples of the recommendations are given in 4.7.

### 4.6.2. Author's name

Take the author's name from the first page or the last page of the article and follow the recommendations for citing names of authors of books (4.4.2).

### 4.6.3. Title of the article

Give the title of the article in full, enclosed in quotation marks (not underlined). Unless the title has its own concluding punctuation (e.g., a question mark), put a period before the closing quotation mark. Follow the recommendations for titles given in 2.5.

### 4.6.4. Name of the periodical

When citing a periodical, omit any introductory article but otherwise give the name, underlined, as it appears on the title page: *William and Mary Quarterly* (not *The William and Mary Quarterly*). Give the city or institution in square brackets to locate an unfamiliar journal or to distinguish a periodical from another with the same name. For newspaper titles, see 4.7.6.

### 4.6.5. Series number or name

If you list a periodical that has appeared in more than one series, state the number or name of the series after the journal title (see 4.7.3).

### 4.6.6. Volume number

Do not precede the volume number with the abbreviation "vol." Although published several times a year (four issues is common), most scholarly journals use continuous pagination throughout each annual volume (see 4.7.1). Some periodicals, however, page issues independent-

ly; others use issue numbers alone and do not have volume numbers (see
4.7.2).

### 4.6.7.  Date of publication

Leave a space after the volume number and give the year of publication, in parentheses, followed by a colon, a space, and the inclusive page
numbers of the article.

<u>College Literature</u> 8 (1981): 85-87.

For daily, weekly, or monthly periodicals omit volume and issue numbers and give the complete date instead, followed by a colon, a space,
and the page number(s). Abbreviate all months except May, June, and
July.

<u>Folio</u> Jan. 1980: 29-31.

<u>Publishers Weekly</u> 19 Feb. 1982: 6-7.

To cite editions of newspapers, see 4.7.6.

### 4.6.8.  Page numbers

Using the rules for writing inclusive numbers (see 2.4.6), give the
pages for the complete article, not just the pages used. (Specific page
references appear parenthetically at appropriate places in your text; see
ch. 5.) Give the page reference for the first page exactly as it appears in
the source: 198–232, A32–34, 28/WETA–29, TV-15–18, lxii–lxv. A period follows the page numbers, concluding the entry. When an article is
not printed on consecutive pages—if, for example, it begins on page 6,
then skips to page 10, and continues on page 22—write only the first
page number and a plus sign, leaving no intervening space (e.g., 6+).

Hook, Janet.  "Raise Standards of Admission,

　　　Colleges Urged." <u>Chronicle of Higher</u>

　　　<u>Education</u> 4 May 1983: 1+.

To cite section numbers of newspapers, see 4.7.6.

## 4.7.  Sample entries: Articles in periodicals

The following examples illustrate the recommendations in 4.6.

### 4.7.1. An article in a journal with continuous pagination

A bibliographic reference to an article in a periodical typically begins with the author's name, the title of the article, and the name of the journal. If the article you are citing appears in a journal with continuous pagination throughout the annual volume (i.e., if the first issue ends on page 130, the next one begins on page 131, etc.), give the volume number followed by the year of publication (in parentheses), a colon, and the inclusive page numbers.

Clark, Herbert H., and Thomas H. Carlson.

"Hearers and Speech Acts." <u>Language</u> 58

(1982): 332-73.                        *volume no.*

Ramsey, Jarold W.  "The Wife Who Goes Out like a

Man, Comes Back as a Hero: The Art of Two

Oregon Indian Narratives." <u>PMLA</u> 92 (1977):

9-18.

Spear, Karen.  "Building Cognitive Skills in Basic

Writers." <u>Teaching English in the Two-Year

College</u> 9 (1983): 91-98.

### 4.7.2. An article in a journal that pages each issue separately or that uses only issue numbers

For a journal that does not number pages continuously throughout an annual volume but begins each issue on page 1, add a period and the issue number, without any intervening space, directly after the volume number (e.g., 14.2, signifying volume 14, issue 2; 10.3-4, for volume 10, issues 3 and 4 combined).

Barthelme, Frederick.  "Architecture." <u>Kansas</u>

<u>Quarterly</u> 13.3-4 (1981): 77-80.

Lyon, George Ella. "Contemporary Appalachian

Poetry: Sources and Directions." <u>Kentucky</u>

<u>Review</u> 2.2 (1981): 3-22.

Monk, Patricia. "Frankenstein's Daughters: The

Problems of the Feminine Image in Science

Fiction." <u>Mosaic</u> 13.3-4 (1980): 15-27.

In citing a journal that uses only issue numbers, treat the issue number as you would a volume number.

Pritchard, Allan. "West of the Great Divide: A

View of the Literature of British Columbia."

<u>Canadian Literature</u> 94 (1982): 96-112.

Wilson, Katharina M. "Tertullian's <u>De cultu</u>

<u>foeminarum</u> and Utopia." <u>Moreana</u> 73 (1982):

69-74.

### 4.7.3. An article from a journal with more than one series

In citing a journal with numbered series, write the number (an arabic digit with the appropriate suffix: 2nd, 3rd, 4th, etc.) and the abbreviation "ser." between the journal title and the volume number (see sample entry for "Johnson"). For a journal divided into a new series and an original series, indicate the series with "ns" or "os," skip a space, and give the volume number (see sample entry for "Avery").

Avery, Robert. "Foreign Influence on the Nautical

Terminology of Russian in the Eighteenth

Century." <u>Oxford Slavonic Papers</u> ns 14

(1981): 73-92.

Johnson, Michael P.  "Runaway Slaves and the Slave

Communities in South Carolina, 1799-1830."

<u>William and Mary Quarterly</u> 3rd ser. 38

(1981): 418-41.

*volume no.*

## 4.7.4.  An article from a weekly or biweekly periodical

In citing a periodical published every week or every two weeks, give the complete date (beginning with the day and abbreviating the month) instead of the volume and issue numbers.

Begley, Sharon.  "A Healthy Dose of Laughter."

<u>Newsweek</u> 4 Oct. 1982: 74.

McDonald, Kim.  "Space Shuttle <u>Columbia</u>'s

Weightless Laboratory Attracts Research."

<u>Chronicle of Higher Education</u> 28 Oct. 1981:

6-7.

Motulsky, Arno G.  "Impact of Genetic Manipulation

on Society and Medicine." <u>Science</u> 14 Jan.

1983: 135-40.

## 4.7.5.  An article from a monthly or bimonthly periodical

In citing a periodical published every month or every two months, give the month(s) and year instead of the volume number and issue.

Corcoran, Elizabeth.  "Space and the Arts." <u>Space</u>

<u>World</u> Oct. 1982: 14+.

Ratcliffe, Carter.  "Where a Visionary Opened His

Eyes: A Fresh Look at El Greco."  <u>Saturday</u>

<u>Review</u> Mar.-Apr. 1983: 24-27.

Snyder, Mark.  "Self-Fulfilling Stereotypes."

<u>Psychology Today</u> July 1982: 60-68.

Tucker, W. Henry.  "Dilemma in Teaching

Engineering Ethics."  <u>Chemical Engineering</u>

<u>Progress</u> Apr. 1983: 20-25.

## 4.7.6.  An article from a daily newspaper

In citing a daily newspaper, give the name as it appears on the masthead but omit any introductory article: *New York Times* (not *The New York Times*). If the city of publication is not included in the name of the newspaper, add it in square brackets, not underlined, after the name: *Star-Ledger* [Newark, NJ]. Next, give the complete date—day, month (abbreviated), and year—instead of the volume and issue numbers.

Because different editions of newspapers contain different material, specify the edition (if one is given on the masthead), preceded by a comma, after the date:

Collins, Glenn.  "Single-Father Survey Finds

Adjustment a Problem."  <u>New York Times</u> 21

Nov. 1983, late ed.: B17.

or

Collins, Glenn.  "Single-Father Survey Finds

Adjustment a Problem."  <u>New York Times</u> 21

Nov. 1983, natl. ed.: 20.

If each section is paginated separately, indicate the appropriate section number or letter. Determining how to indicate a section, however, can sometimes be complicated. The *New York Times*, for example, currently designates sections in three separate ways, depending on the day of the week. On Monday through Friday, there are normally four sections, labeled A, B, C, and D and paginated separately, with each page number preceded by the section letter (e.g., A1, B1, C5, D3). On Saturday, the paper is not divided into specific sections, and pagination is continuous, from the first page to the last. (The daily national edition follows the same practice.) Finally, the Sunday edition contains several individually paged sections (travel, arts and leisure, book review, business, sports, magazine, and others), designated not by letters but by numbers, which do not appear as parts of the page numbers. Each system calls for a different method of indicating section and page.

If the newspaper is not divided into sections, give the page number after the date, the edition (if one is stated on the masthead), a colon, and a space (see sample entry for "Dalin"). If the pagination includes a section designation, give the page number as it appears (e.g., C1; see sample entries for "Greenberg" and "Schreiner"). If the section designation is not part of the pagination, put a comma after the date (and, if any, the edition) and add the abbreviation "sec.," the appropriate letter or number, a colon, and the page number (see sample entry for "Kerr").

Dalin, Damon.   "A $7 Greeting Card? Yes, but

　　　Listen to the Melody It Will Play for You."

　　　Wall Street Journal 10 May 1983, eastern ed.:

　　　37.

Greenberg, Daniel S.   "Ridding American Politics

　　　of Polls."  Washington Post 16 Sept. 1980:

　　　A17.

Kerr, Walter.  "When One Inspired Gesture

　　　Illuminates the Stage."  New York Times 8

　　　Jan. 1984, late ed., sec. 2: 1+.

```
Schreiner, Tim.  "Future Is A) Dim or B) Bright

    (Pick One)."  USA Today 2 June 1983: 3A.
```

### 4.7.7. An editorial

If you are citing a signed editorial, begin with the author's name, give the title, and then add the descriptive label "Editorial," neither underlined nor enclosed in quotation marks. Conclude with the appropriate publication information. If the editorial is unsigned, begin with the title and continue in the same way.

```
Malkofsky, Morton.  "Let the Unions Negotiate

    What's Negotiable."  Editorial.  Learning

     Oct. 1982: 6.

"An Uneasy Silence."  Editorial.  Computerworld

    28 Mar. 1983: 54.
```

### 4.7.8. An anonymous article

If no author's name is given for the article you are citing, begin the entry with the title and alphabetize by title.

```
"Portents for Future Learning."  Time 21 Sept.

    1981: 65.

"The Starry Sky."  Odyssey Jan. 1984: 26-27.
```

### 4.7.9. A letter to the editor

To identify a letter to the editor, write "Letter" after the name of the author, but do not underline the word or place it in quotation marks.

```
Levin, Harry.  Letter.  Partisan Review 47 (1980):

    320.
```

If an author has replied to a letter, identify the response as "Reply to letter of . . ." and add the name of the writer of the initial letter. Do not underline this information or place it in quotation marks.

Patai, Daphne.  Reply to letter of Erwin Hester.

    PMLA 98 (1983): 257-58.

## 4.7.10.  A review

   In citing a review, give the reviewer's name and the title of the review (if there is one); then write "Rev. of" (neither underlined nor placed in quotation marks), the title of the work reviewed, a comma, the word "by," and the name of the author. If the work of an editor or translator is under review, use "ed." or "trans." instead of "by." For the review of a performance, add pertinent information about the production (see sample entry for "Henahan"). Conclude with the name of the periodical and the rest of the publication information.

   If the review is titled but unsigned, begin the entry with the title of the review and alphabetize by that title (see sample entry for "The Cooling of an Admiration"). If the review is neither titled nor signed, begin the entry with "Rev. of" and alphabetize under the title of the work being reviewed (see sample entry for *Anthology of Danish Literature*).

Rev. of Anthology of Danish Literature, ed. F. J.

    Billeskov Jansen and P. M. Mitchell. Times

    Literary Supplement 7 July 1972: 785.

Ashton, Sherley.  Rev. of Death and Dying, by

    David L. Bender and Richard C. Hagen.

    Humanist July-Aug. 1982: 60.

"The Cooling of an Admiration."  Rev. of

    Pound/Joyce: The Letters of Ezra Pound to

    James Joyce, ed. Forrest Read.  Times

    Literary Supplement 6 Mar. 1969: 239-40.

Edwards, R. Dudley.  Rev. of The Dissolution of

<u>the Religious Orders in Ireland under Henry</u>

<u>VIII</u>, by Brendan Bradshaw.  <u>Renaissance</u>

<u>Quarterly</u> 29 (1976): 401-03.

Henahan, Donal.  Rev. of <u>Rinaldo</u>, by George

Frideric Handel.  Metropolitan Opera, New

York.  <u>New York Times</u> 21 Jan. 1984, late ed.:

9.

Updike, John.  "Cohn's Doom."  Rev. of <u>God's</u>

<u>Grace</u>, by Bernard Malamud.  <u>New Yorker</u> 8 Nov.

1982: 167-70.

## 4.7.11.  An article whose title contains a quotation or a title within quotation marks

If the title of the article you are citing contains a quotation or a title within quotation marks, use single quotation marks around the quotation or the shorter title (see 2.5.4).

Carrier, Warren.  "Commonplace Costumes and

Essential Gaudiness: Wallace Stevens' 'The

Emperor of Ice Cream.'"  <u>College Literature</u> 1

(1974): 230-35.

Duncan-Jones, E. E.  "Moore's 'A Kiss à l'Antique'

and Keats's 'Ode on a Grecian Urn.'"  <u>Notes</u>

<u>and Queries</u> ns 28 (1981): 316-17.

Nitzsche, Jane Chance.  "'As swete as is the roote

of lycorys, or any cetewale': Herbal Imagery

in Chaucer's Miller's Tale." <u>Chaucer</u>

<u>Newsletter</u> 2.1 (1980): 6-8.

## 4.7.12. An abstract from *Dissertation Abstracts* or *Dissertation Abstracts International*

Beginning with volume 30 (1969), *Dissertation Abstracts* (*DA*) became *Dissertation Abstracts International* (*DAI*). From volume 27 to volume 36, *DA* and *DAI* were paginated in two series: "A" for humanities and social sciences, "B" for the sciences. With volume 37, *DAI* added a third separately paginated section: "C" for abstracts of European dissertations. Identify the degree-granting institution at the end of a *DA* or *DAI* entry (for citing dissertations themselves, see 4.5.26–27).

Gans, Eric L.  "The Discovery of Illusion:

Flaubert's Early Works, 1835-1837." <u>DA</u> 27

(1967): 3046A.  Johns Hopkins U.

Johnson, Nancy Kay.  "Cultural and Psychosocial

Determinants of Health and Illness." <u>DAI</u> 40

(1980): 4235B.  U of Washington.

Norris, Christine Lynn.  "Literary Allusion in the

Tales of Isak Dinesen." <u>DAI</u> 43 (1982):

453A.  U of California, San Diego.

## 4.7.13. A serialized article

To cite a serialized article or a series of related articles published in more than one issue of a periodical, include all bibliographic information in one entry if each installment has the same author and title.

Gillespie, Gerald.  "Novella, Nouvelle, Novelle,

Short Novel? A Review of Terms."

<u>Neophilologus</u> 51 (1967): 117-27, 225-30.

Meserole, Harrison T., and James M. Rambeau.

"Articles on American Literature Appearing in

Current Periodicals." <u>American Literature</u> 52

(1981): 688-705; 53 (1981): 164-80, 348-59.

If the installments bear different titles, list each one separately. You may include a brief description at the end of the entry to indicate that the article is part of a series.

Gottlieb, Martin. "Pressure and Compromise Saved

Times Square Project." <u>New York Times</u> 10

Mar. 1984, late ed.: 25. Pt. 2 of a series

begun on 9 Mar. 1984.

---. "Times Square Development Plan: A Lesson in

Politics and Power." <u>New York Times</u> 9 Mar.

1984, late ed.: B1. Pt. 1 of a series.

## 4.8. Sample entries: Other sources

### 4.8.1. Computer software

An entry for a commercially produced computer program should contain the following information: the writer of the program, if known; the title of the program, underlined; the descriptive label "Computer software," neither underlined nor enclosed in quotation marks; the distributor; and the year of publication. Put a period after each item except the distributor, which is followed by a comma. At the end of the entry add any other pertinent information—for example, the computer for which the program is designed (e.g., Apple, Atari, or VIC); the number of kilobytes, or units of memory (e.g., 8KB); the operating system (e.g., IBM PC-DOS 2.10, CP/M 2.2); and the form of the program (e.g., cartridge, cassette, or disk). Separate these items with commas and conclude the entry with a period.

<u>Connections</u>. Computer software. Krell Software,

     1982.

Kilgus, Robert G. <u>Color Scripsit</u>. Computer

     software. Tandy, 1981. TRS-80, cartridge.

Pattis, Richard E. <u>Karel the Robot: A Gentle</u>

     <u>Introduction to the Art of Programming</u>.

     Computer software. Cybertronics, 1981.

Starks, Sparky. <u>Diskey</u>. Computer software.

     Adventure, 1982. Atari 400/800, 32KB, disk.

White, Jerry. <u>Music Lessons</u>. Computer software.

     Swifty Software, 1981.

## 4.8.2. Material from a computer service

Treat material obtained from a computer service—such as BRS, DI-ALOG, or Mead—like other printed material, but add a reference to the service at the end of the entry. Give the publication information as provided by the service, the name of the vendor providing the service, and the accession or identifying numbers within the service.

Schomer, Howard. "South Africa: Beyond Fair

     Employment." <u>Harvard Business Review</u>

     May-June 1983: 145+. DIALOG file 122, item

     119425 833160.

"Turner, Barbara Bush." <u>American Men and Women of</u>

     <u>Science</u>. 15th ed. Bowker, 1983. DIALOG

     file 236, item 0107406.

```
File122:Harvard Business Review - 1971-84,Jan/Feb
(Copr. Harvard 1984)


119425       833160       **COMPLETE TEXT AVAILABLE**
South Africa: Beyond Fair Employment
Schomer, Howard - Howard Schomer Associates - United Church of Christ
HARVARD BUSINESS REVIEW, May/Jun 1983, p. 145


TEXT:
Executives  of  companies  with interests in South Africa have known for
some time that neutrality toward the government's policy of apartheid is at
least irresponsible,  if not downright dishonest.  Few actually agree  with
the notion that enshrining white supremacy as a constitutional principle is
a defensible political course.
     And  so  they've  done something about it.  When the government of Prime
Minister Pieter Botha allowed limited yet independent black unions in 1979,
for  example,  some  companies  immediately  began  to  negotiate  with
representatives  of  blacks  and  bypassed  the  government-supported labor
organizations,  which are dominated by whites.  Fully 30% of the 400  U.S.
companies  with  affiliates  or  subsidiaries  in South Africa have committed
themselves to racial equality in their operations,  in accordance with  six
principles  promulgated  in  1977  by  the Reverend Leon Sullivan,  a black
social reformer who has become a  member  of  the  board  of  directors  of
General Motors (for more details on the Sullivan initiative,  see the ruled
insert).
     But are such actions by companies enough? Absolutely not.  Events of the
last  few years cause knowledgeable corporate executives to despair whether
the white rulers of South Africa will be able to move swiftly enough toward
equal rights for all. No longer can they think that the problem will simply
go away or that the government can indefinitely contain the black drive for
equality.  The much-heralded initiative to allow independent black  unions,
taken  after  a 1976 police assault on unarmed demonstrators in Soweto that
resulted in 600 deaths, 6,000 arrests, and hundreds of banning orders,  has
been followed in 1980 to 1982 by a climate of renewed repression in which:
     More  than  a  dozen trade union leaders have been held for long periods
without trial for questioning.
     Ten prisoners have reportedly committed suicide while being held without
charge or trial under the stringent security laws.
     An unprecedented court inquiry into the  mysterious  death  of  a  white
prisoner,  Dr.  Neil Aggett,  while formally exonerating prison officials,
pointed up the kinds of torture the government uses as standard practice.
     Black political groups,  like the African National Congress,  have been
systematically banned,  and white workers for black unions,  like Barbara
Anne Hogan, have been sentenced to ten years imprisonment for high treason.
```

*The beginning of an article from* Harvard Business Review *as retrieved from DIALOG. Entering the appropriate file number (122) yields a note on the holdings available. Having searched the entire holdings for appropriate terms, the system retrieved this article.*

## 4.8.3.  Material from an information service

Treat material obtained from an information service—such as ERIC (Educational Resources Information Center) or NTIS (National Technical Information Service)—like other printed material, but add a reference to the service at the end of the entry. If the material was published previously, give the full details of its original publication, followed by the name of the service and the identifying number within the service.

```
Phillips, June K., ed.  Action for the '80s: A

Political, Professional, and Public Program
```

for Foreign Language Education. Skokie:

Natl. Textbook, 1981. ERIC ED 197 599.

Spolsky, Bernard. Navajo Language Maintenance:

Six-Year-Olds in 1969. Navajo Reading Study

Prog. Rept. 5. Albuquerque: U of New Mexico,

1969. ERIC ED 043 004.

If the material was not previously published, treat its distribution by the information service as the mode of publication.

Streiff, Paul R. Some Criteria for Designing

Evaluation of TESOL Programs. ERIC, 1970.

ED 040 385.

No place of publication is cited for materials distributed by the ERIC Document Reproduction Service (EDRS), since the location of this government-sponsored service changes.

## 4.8.4. Radio and television programs

The information for an entry for a radio or television program usually appears in the following order: the title of the program, underlined; the network (e.g., PBS); the local station and its city (e.g., KETC, St. Louis); and the date of broadcast. Where appropriate, the title of the episode, in quotation marks, should precede the title of the program, and the title of the series, neither underlined nor enclosed in quotation marks, should appear after the program (see sample entry for "The Joy Ride"). Use commas between the station and the city, periods after all other items. For the inclusion of other information that may be pertinent (e.g., director, narrator, producer), see the sample entries.

Boris Godunov. By Modest Mussorgsky. With Martti

Talvela. Cond. James Conlon. Metropolitan

Opera. Texaco-Metropolitan Opera Radio

Network.  WGAU, Athens, GA.  29 Jan. 1983.

The First Americans.  Narr. Hugh Downs.  Writ. and
prod. Craig Fisher.  NBC News Special.  KNBC,
Los Angeles.  21 Mar. 1968.

Götterdämmerung.  By Richard Wagner.  Dir. Patrice
Chereau.  With Gwyneth Jones and Manfred
Jung.  Cond. Pierre Boulez.  Bayreuth
Festival Orch.  PBS.  WNET, New York.  6 and
13 June 1983.

"The Joy Ride."  Writ. Alfred Shaughnessy.
Upstairs, Downstairs.  Created by Eileen
Atkins and Jean Marsh.  Dir. Bill Bain.
Prod. John Hawkesworth.  Masterpiece
Theatre.  Introd. Alistair Cooke.  PBS.
WGBH, Boston.  6 Feb. 1977.

If your reference is primarily to the work of a particular individual, cite
that person's name before the title.

Dickens, Charles.  The Life and Adventures of
Nicholas Nickleby.  Adapt. David Edgar.  Dir.
Trevor Nunn and John Caird.  With Roger Rees
and Emily Richard.  Royal Shakespeare Co.
Mobil Showcase Network.  WNEW, New York.

10-13 Jan. 1983.

Welles, Orson, dir. <u>War of the Worlds</u>. Writ.

>   Howard Koch. Based on H. G. Wells's <u>War of</u>

>   <u>the Worlds</u>. Mercury Theatre on the Air. CBS

>   Radio. WCBS, New York. 30 Oct. 1938.

See 4.8.11 for interviews on radio and television programs; see 4.8.5 for recordings and 4.8.7 for performances.

## 4.8.5. Recordings

In an entry for a commercially available recording the person cited first (e.g., the composer, conductor, or performer) will depend on the desired emphasis. Include the title of the record or tape (or the titles of the works included), the artist(s), the manufacturer, the catalog number, and the year of issue (if unknown, write "n.d."). Commas follow the manufacturer and the number; periods follow other items. If you are using a tape recording, indicate the medium (e.g., Audiotape), neither underlined nor placed in quotation marks, immediately after the title (see sample entries for "Eliot" and "Wilgus"). Include physical characteristics at the end of the entry if the information is relevant or if the recording is not readily available (see sample entry for "Wilgus").

If the title of a recording of classical music is less important than the list of works recorded, omit it from the citation. In general, underline record titles, but do not underline or put in quotation marks the titles of musical compositions identified only by form, number, and key (see 2.5.2 as well as the sample entries for "Beethoven" and "Mozart"). You may wish to indicate, in addition to the year of issue, the actual date of recording (see sample entries for "Ellington" and "Holiday").

Beethoven, Ludwig van. Symphony no. 7 in A, op.

>   92. Cond. Herbert von Karajan. Vienna

>   Philharmonic Orch. London, STS 15107, 1966.

Berlioz, Hector. <u>Symphonie fantastique</u>, op. 14.

>   Cond. Georg Solti. Chicago Symphony Orch.

London, CS 6790, 1968.

Ellington, Duke, cond. Duke Ellington Orch.
<u>First Carnegie Hall Concert</u>. Rec. 23 Jan.
1943. Prestige, P-34004, 1977.

Falla, Manuel de. <u>Quatre pièces espagnoles</u>, Dance
no. 2 from <u>La vida breve</u>, "Danza de los
vecinos" and "Danza de la molinera" from <u>El
sombrero de tres picos</u>, "Danza del terror"
from <u>El amor brujo</u>, and <u>Fantasía bética</u>.
Alicia de Larrocha, pianist. Turnabout-Vox,
TVS 34742, 1978.

Holiday, Billie. "God Bless the Child." Rec. 9
May 1941. <u>Billie Holiday: The Golden Years</u>.
Columbia, C3L 21, 1962.

Joplin, Scott. <u>Treemonisha</u>. With Carmen
Balthrop, Betty Allen, and Curtis Rayam.
Cond. Gunther Schuller. Houston Grand Opera
Orch. and Chorus. Deutsche Grammophon,
S-2707 083, 1975.

Lloyd Webber, Andrew. <u>Cats</u>. With Elaine Page and
Brian Blessed. Cond. David Firman. Geffen,
2GHS 2017, 1981.

Mozart, Wolfgang A.  Symphony no. 35 in D and

     Overtures to <u>The Marriage of Figaro</u>, <u>The</u>

     <u>Magic Flute</u>, and <u>Don Giovanni</u>.  Cond. Antonia

     Brico.  Mostly Mozart Orch.  Columbia,

     M33888, 1976.

Sondheim, Stephen.  <u>Sweeney Todd</u>.  With Angela

     Lansbury and Len Cariou.  Cond. Paul

     Gemignani.  RCA, CBL2-3379, 1979.

Verdi, Giuseppe.  <u>Rigoletto</u>.  With Joan

     Sutherland, Luciano Pavarotti, Sherrill

     Milnes, and Martti Talvela.  Cond. Richard

     Bonynge.  London Symphony Orch. and Ambrosian

     Opera Chorus.  London, OSA-12105, 1973.

   Treat a recording of the spoken word as you would a musical record-ing. Begin with the speaker, the writer, or the production director, de-pending on the desired emphasis.

Eliot, T. S.  <u>Old Possum's Book of Practical</u>

     <u>Cats</u>.  Audiotape.  Read by John Gielgud and

     Irene Worth.  Caedmon, CP 1713, 1983.

Frost, Robert.  "The Road Not Taken." <u>Robert</u>

     <u>Frost Reads His Poetry</u>.  Caedmon, TC 1060,

     1956.

Lehmann, Lotte. <u>Lotte Lehmann Reading German</u>

<u>Poetry</u>. Caedmon, TC 1072, 1958.

Murrow, Edward R. <u>Year of Decision: 1943</u>.

Columbia, CPS-3872, 1957.

Shakespeare, William. <u>Othello</u>. Dir. John

Dexter. With Laurence Olivier, Maggie Smith,

Frank Finley, and Derek Jacobi. RCA,

VDM-100, 1964.

Welles, Orson, dir. <u>War of the Worlds</u>. Writ.

Howard Koch. Based on H. G. Wells's <u>War of</u>

<u>the Worlds</u>. Mercury Theatre on the Air.

Rec. 30 Oct. 1938. Evolution, 4001, 1969.

Do not underline or enclose in quotation marks the title of a private or archival recording or tape. Include the date recorded (if known), the location and identifying number of the recording, and the physical characteristics (if ascertainable).

Wilgus, D. K. Southern Folk Tales. Audiotape.

Rec. 23-25 Mar. 1965. U of California, Los

Angeles, Archives of Folklore. B.76.82.

7 1/2 ips, 7" reel.

In citing the jacket notes, libretto, or other material accompanying a recording, give the author's name, the title of the material (if any), and a description of the material (e.g., Jacket notes, Libretto). Then provide the usual bibliographic information for a recording.

Colette. Libretto. <u>L'enfant et les sortilèges</u>.

Music by Maurice Ravel.  With Suzanne Danco

and Hugues Cuenod.  Cond. Ernest Ansermet.

Orch. de la Suisse Romande.  Richmond-London,

SR 33086, n.d.

Collins, Judy.  Jacket notes.  Antonia Brico,

cond.  Mostly Mozart Orch.  Symphony no. 35

in D and Overtures to The Marriage of Figaro,

The Magic Flute, and Don Giovanni.  By

Wolfgang A. Mozart.  Columbia, M33888, 1976.

Lawrence, Vera Brodsky.  "Scott Joplin and

Treemonisha."  Libretto.  Treemonisha.  By

Scott Joplin.  Deutsche Grammophon, S-2707

083, 1975.  10-12.

Lewiston, David.  Jacket notes.  The Balinese

Gamelan: Music from the Morning of the

World.  Nonesuch Explorer Series, H-2015,

n.d.

## 4.8.6.  Films, filmstrips, slide programs, and videotapes

A film citation usually begins with the title, underlined, and includes the director, the distributor, and the year. You may include other data if they seem pertinent: information such as the writer, performers, and producer would follow the title; physical characteristics, such as the size and length of the film, would go after the date.

<u>A bout de souffle</u> [<u>Breathless</u>].  Dir. Jean-Luc

    Godard.  With Jean-Paul Belmondo and Jean

    Seberg.  Beauregard, 1960.

<u>Det Sjunde Inseglet</u> [<u>The Seventh Seal</u>].  Dir.

    Ingmar Bergman.  Svensk Filmindustri, 1956.

If you are citing the contribution of a particular individual, begin with
that person's name.

Chaplin, Charles, dir.  <u>Modern Times</u>.  With

    Chaplin and Paulette Goddard.  United

    Artists, 1936.

Lerner, Alan Jay, screenwriter.  <u>An American in</u>

    <u>Paris</u>.  Dir. Vincente Minnelli.  Prod. Arthur

    Freed.  Music by George Gershwin.  Lyrics by

    Ira Gershwin.  With Gene Kelly, Leslie Caron,

    and Oscar Levant.  MGM, 1951.

Mifune, Toshiro, actor.  <u>Rashomon</u>.  Dir. Akira

    Kurosawa.  With Machiko Kyo.  Daiei, 1950.

Rota, Nino, composer.  <u>Giulietta degli spiriti</u>

    [<u>Juliet of the Spirits</u>].  Dir. Federico

    Fellini.  With Giulietta Masina.  Rizzoli,

    1965.

In citing a filmstrip, slide program, or videotape, include the medium, neither underlined nor enclosed in quotation marks, immediately

after the title and then give the usual bibliographic information for films.

Alcohol Use and Its Medical Consequences: A

    Comprehensive Teaching Program for Biomedical

    Education. Slide program. Developed by

    Project Cork, Dartmouth Medical School.

    Milner-Fenwick, 1982. 46 slides.

Consumer Awareness: Supply, Demand, Competition,

    and Prices. Sound filmstrip. Prod. Visual

    Education. Maclean Hunter Learning

    Resources, 1981. 85 fr., 11 min.

Creation vs. Evolution: "Battle of the

    Classroom." Videocassette. Dir. Ryall

    Wilson. PBS Video, 1982. 58 min.

## 4.8.7. Performances

An entry for a performance (e.g., a stage play, opera, ballet, or concert) usually begins with the title, contains information similar to that for a film (see 4.8.6), and concludes with the theater and city, separated by a comma and followed by a period, and the date of the performance.

Boris Godunov. By Modest Mussorgsky. Dir. August

    Everding. Cond. James Conlon. With Martti

    Talvela. Metropolitan Opera. Metropolitan

    Opera House, New York. 29 Jan. 1983.

<u>Cats</u>. By Andrew Lloyd Webber. Based on T. S.

    Eliot's <u>Old Possum's Book of Practical Cats</u>.

    Dir. Trevor Nunn. New London Theatre,

    London. 11 May 1981.

<u>La Fanciulla del West</u>. By Giacomo Puccini. Dir.

    Patrick Bakman. Cond. Stefan Minde. With

    Marilyn Zschau and Vladimir Popov. Portland

    Opera Assn. Civic Auditorium, Portland, OR.

    17 Mar. 1983.

<u>Hamlet</u>. By William Shakespeare. Dir. John

    Gielgud. With Richard Burton. Shubert

    Theatre, Boston. 4 Mar. 1964.

If you are citing the contribution of a particular individual, begin with that person's name.

Balanchine, George, chor. <u>Mozartiana</u>. With

    Suzanne Farrell. New York City Ballet. New

    York State Theater, New York. 20 Nov. 1981.

Caldwell, Sarah, dir. and cond. <u>La Traviata</u>. By

    Giuseppe Verdi. With Beverly Sills. Opera

    Co. of Boston. Orpheum Theatre, Boston. 4

    Nov. 1972.

Ellington, Duke, cond.  Duke Ellington Orch.

> Concert.  Carnegie Hall, New York.  23 Jan.

> 1943.

Joplin, Scott.  <u>Treemonisha</u>.  Dir. Frank Corsaro.

> Cond. Gunther Schuller.  With Carmen

> Balthrop, Betty Allen, and Curtis Rayam.

> Houston Grand Opera.  Miller Theatre,

> Houston.  18 May 1975.

Prince, Harold, dir.  <u>Sweeney Todd</u>.  By Stephen

> Sondheim.  With Angela Lansbury and Len

> Cariou.  Uris Theatre, New York.  1 Mar.

> 1979.

Shaw, Robert, cond.  Atlanta Symphony Orch.

> Concert.  Atlanta Arts Center, Atlanta.  14

> Dec. 1981.

For broadcasts and telecasts of performances, see 4.8.4; for recordings of performances, see 4.8.5.

## 4.8.8.  Musical compositions

In citing a musical composition, begin with the composer's name. Underline the title of an opera, a ballet, or instrumental music identified by name (e.g., *Symphonie fantastique*), but do not underline or put in quotation marks an instrumental composition identified only by form, number, and key.

Beethoven, Ludwig van.  Symphony no. 7 in A, op.

> 92.

Berlioz, Hector.  <u>Symphonie fantastique</u>, op. 14.

Wagner, Richard.  <u>Götterdämmerung</u>.

Treat a published score, however, like a book. Give the title as it appears on the title page and underline it.

Beethoven, Ludwig van.  <u>Symphony No. 7 in A, Op.</u>

    <u>92</u>.  Kalmus Miniature Orchestra Scores 7.

    New York: Kalmus, n.d.

For recordings of musical compositions, see 4.8.5; see 4.8.4 for radio and television programs and 4.8.7 for performances.

## 4.8.9.  Works of art

In citing a work of art, state the artist's name first. In general, underline the title of a painting or sculpture. Name the institution housing the work (e.g., a museum), followed by a comma and the city.

Bernini, Gianlorenzo.  <u>Ecstasy of St. Teresa</u>.

    Santa Maria della Vittoria, Rome.

Rembrandt van Rijn.  <u>Aristotle Contemplating the</u>

    <u>Bust of Homer</u>.  Metropolitan Museum of Art,

    New York.

If you use a photograph of the work, indicate not only the institution and the city but also the complete publication information for the work in which the photograph appears.

Cassatt, Mary.  <u>Mother and Child</u>.  Wichita Art

    Museum, Wichita.  Slide 22 of <u>American</u>

    <u>Painting: 1560-1913</u>.  By John Pearce.  New

    York: McGraw, 1964.

Houdon, Jean-Antoine. <u>Statue of Voltaire</u>.

Comédie Française, Paris. Illus. 51 in

<u>Literature through Art: A New Approach to</u>

<u>French Literature</u>. By Helmut A. Hatzfeld.

New York: Oxford UP, 1952.

## 4.8.10.  Letters

As bibliographic entries, letters fall into three general categories: (1) published letters, (2) letters in archives, and (3) letters received by the researcher. Treat a published letter like a work in a collection (see 4.5.8), adding the date of the letter and the number (if the editor has assigned one).

Thackeray, William Makepeace.  "To George Henry

Lewes."  6 Mar. 1848.  Letter 452 in <u>Letters</u>

<u>and Private Papers of William Makepeace</u>

<u>Thackeray</u>.  Ed. Gordon N. Ray.  4 vols.

Cambridge: Harvard UP, 1946.  2: 353-54.

If you are citing more than one letter from a published collection, however, provide a single entry for the entire work and give individual citations in the text (see 4.5.10).

In citing unpublished letters, follow the basic guidelines for manuscripts and typescripts (see 4.8.15) and for private and archival recordings and tapes (see 4.8.5).

Benton, Thomas Hart.  Letter to John Charles

Fremont.  22 June 1847.  John Charles Fremont

Papers.  Southwest Museum Library, Los

Angeles.

Cite a letter personally received as follows:

Copland, Aaron.  Letter to the author.  17 May

    1982.

## 4.8.11.  Interviews

Interviews fall into a number of categories: (1) published or recorded interviews, (2) interviews on radio or television, and (3) interviews conducted by the researcher. Begin with the name of the person interviewed. If the interview is part of a publication, recording, or program, put the title, if any, in quotation marks; if the interview is the entire work, underline the title. If the interview is untitled, use the descriptive label "Interview," neither underlined nor enclosed in quotation marks. (Interviewers' names may be included if known and if pertinent; see sample entry below for "Stravinsky.") Conclude with the usual bibliographic information required for the entry.

Fellini, Federico.  "The Long Interview."  <u>Juliet</u>

    <u>of the Spirits</u>.  Ed. Tullio Kezich.  Trans.

    Howard Greenfield.  New York: Ballantine,

    1966.  17-64.

Gordon, Suzanne.  Interview.  <u>All Things</u>

    <u>Considered</u>.  Natl. Public Radio.  WNYC, New

    York.  1 June 1983.

Kundera, Milan.  Interview.  <u>New York Times</u> 18

    Jan. 1982, late ed., sec. 3: 13+.

Stravinsky, Igor.  <u>Conversation with Igor</u>

    <u>Stravinsky</u>.  With Robert Craft.  Berkeley: U

    of California P, 1980.

```
Wolfe, Tom.  Interview.  The Wrong Stuff: American

    Architecture.  Videocassette.  Dir. Tom

    Bettag.  Carousel Films, 1983.
```

In citing a personally conducted interview, give the name of the interviewee, the kind of interview (Personal interview, Telephone interview), and the date.

```
Pei, I. M.  Personal interview.  27 July 1983.

Poussaint, Alvin F.  Telephone interview.  10 Dec.

    1980.
```

### 4.8.12.  Maps and charts

In general, treat maps and charts like anonymous books, but add the appropriate descriptive label (e.g., Map, Chart).

```
Canada.  Map.  Chicago: Rand, 1983.

Grammar and Punctuation.  Chart.  Grand Haven:

    School Zone, 1980.
```

For additional guidance in citing such sources as dioramas, flashcards, games, globes, kits, and models, see Eugene B. Fleischer, *A Style Manual for Citing Microform and Nonprint Media* (Chicago: American Library Assn., 1978).

### 4.8.13.  Cartoons

To cite a cartoon, state the cartoonist's name, the title of the cartoon (if any) in quotation marks, and the descriptive label "Cartoon," neither underlined nor enclosed in quotation marks. Conclude with the usual publication information.

```
Addams, Charles.  Cartoon.  New Yorker 21 Feb.

    1983: 41.

Schulz, Charles.  "Peanuts."  Cartoon.
```

<u>Star-Ledger</u> [Newark, NJ] 4 Sept. 1980: 72.

## 4.8.14. Lectures, speeches, and addresses

Give the speaker's name, the title of the lecture (if known) in quotation marks, the meeting and the sponsoring organization (if applicable), the location, and the date. If there is no title, use an appropriate descriptive label (e.g., Lecture, Address, Keynote speech), neither underlined nor enclosed in quotation marks.

Ciardi, John. Address. Opening General Sess.

NCTE Convention. Washington, 19 Nov. 1982.

Ridley, Florence. "Forget the Past, Reject the

Future: Chaos Is Come Again." Div. on

Teaching of Literature, MLA Convention. Los

Angeles, 28 Dec. 1982.

## 4.8.15. Manuscripts and typescripts

In citing a manuscript or a typescript, state the author, the title (e.g., *La chanson de Roland*) or a description of the material (e.g., Notebook), the form of the material (ms. for manuscript, ts. for typescript), and any identifying number assigned to it. If a library or other research institution houses the material, give its name and location.

<u>La chanson de Roland</u>. Digby ms. 23. Bodleian

Library, Oxford.

Smith, John. "Shakespeare's Dark Lady."

Unpublished essay, 1983.

Twain, Mark. Notebook 32, ts. Mark Twain

Papers. U of California, Berkeley.

## 4.8.16. Legal references

The citation of legal documents and law cases may be complicated. If your paper requires many such references, consult the most recent edition of *A Uniform System of Citation* (Cambridge: Harvard Law Rev. Assn.), an indispensable guide in this field.

In general, do not underline or enclose in quotation marks laws, acts, and similar documents in either the text or the list of works cited (e.g., Declaration of Independence, Constitution of the United States, Taft-Hartley Act). Such works are usually cited by sections, with the year number added if relevant. Although lawyers and legal scholars adopt many abbreviations in their citations, use only familiar abbreviations when writing for a more general audience.

**15 US Code.  Sec. 78j(b).  1964.**

**US Const.  Art. 1, sec. 1**

Note that in references to the United States Code, often abbreviated as USC, the title number precedes the code: 12 USC, 15 USC, etc. Alphabetize under "United States Code" even if you use the abbreviation. When including more than one reference to the code, list individual entries in numerical order.

Names of law cases are both abbreviated and shortened (Brown v. Board of Ed. *for* Oliver Brown versus Board of Education of Topeka, Kansas), but the first important word of each party is always spelled out. Unlike laws, names of cases are underlined in the text but not in bibliographic entries. In citing a case, include, in addition to the names of the first plaintiff and the first defendant, the volume, name, and page (in that order) of the law report cited; the name of the court that decided the case; and the year in which it was decided. Once again, considerable abbreviation is the norm. The following citation, for example, refers to page 755 of volume 148 of the *United States Patent Quarterly* dealing with the case of Stevens against the National Broadcasting Company, which was decided by the California Superior Court in 1966.

**Stevens v. National Broadcasting Co.  148 USPQ**

**755.  Calif. Super. Ct.  1966.**

# 5  DOCUMENTING SOURCES

## 5.1.  What to document

In writing your research paper, you must document everything that you borrow—not only direct quotations and paraphrases but also information and ideas. Of course, common sense as well as ethics should determine what you document. For example, you rarely need to give sources for familiar proverbs ("You can't judge a book by its cover"), well-known quotations ("We shall overcome"), or common knowledge ("George Washington was the first president of the United States"). But you must indicate the source of any borrowed material that readers might otherwise mistake for your own. (On note-taking and plagiarism, see 1.5 and 1.6, respectively.)

## 5.2.  Parenthetical documentation and the list of works cited

The list of works cited at the end of your research paper plays an important role in your acknowledgment of sources (see ch. 4), but it does not in itself provide sufficiently detailed and precise documentation. You must indicate exactly what you have derived from each source and exactly where in that work you found the material. The most practical way to supply this information is to insert brief parenthetical acknowledgments in your paper wherever you incorporate another's words, facts, or ideas. Usually, the author's last name and a page reference are enough to identify the source and the specific location from which you have borrowed material.

Ancient writers attributed the invention of the

monochord to Pythagoras (Marcuse 197).

The parenthetical reference indicates that the information on the monochord comes from page 197 of the book by Marcuse included in the alphabetically arranged list of works cited that follows the text. Thus, it enables the reader to find complete publication information for the source:

Marcuse, Sibyl. _A Survey of Musical Instruments_.

New York: Harper, 1975.

The sample references in 5.5 offer recommendations for documenting many other kinds of sources.

## 5.3.  Information required in parenthetical documentation

In determining the information needed to document sources accurately, keep the following guidelines in mind:

1.   References in the text must clearly point to specific sources in the list of works cited. The information in the parenthetical reference, therefore, must match the corresponding information in the list. When the list contains only one work by the author cited, you need give only the author's last name to identify the work (though you would, of course, have to give the first name as well if two authors on the list had the same last name). If the work has more than one author, give all the last names or one last name followed by "et al.," in keeping with the bibliographic entry (see 5.5.1). If there is a corporate author, use that name, or a shortened version of it (see 5.5.5); if the work is listed by title, use the title, or a shortened version (see 5.5.4); if the list contains more than one work by the author, give the title cited, or a shortened version, after the author's last name (see 5.5.6).

2.   Identify the location of the borrowed information as specifically as possible. Give the relevant page number(s) (see 5.5.2) or, if citing a multivolume work, the volume and page number(s) (see 5.5.3). In references to literary works, it may be appropriate to give information other than, or in addition to, the page numbers—for example, the chapter, the book, the stanza, or the act, scene, and line (see 5.5.8). You may omit page numbers when citing one-page articles, articles in works like encyclopedias that are arranged alphabetically, or, of course, nonprint sources (see 5.5.4).

## 5.4.  Readability

Keep parenthetical references as brief—and as few—as clarity and accuracy permit. Give only the information needed to identify a source and do not add a parenthetical reference unnecessarily. If you are citing an entire work, for example, rather than a specific part of it, the author's name in the text may be the only documentation required. The statement "Booth has devoted an entire book to the subject" needs no parenthetical documentation if the list of works cited includes only one work by Booth. If, for the reader's convenience, you wished to name the book in your text, you could recast the sentence: "In *The Rhetoric of Fiction* Booth deals with this subject exclusively." Remember that there is a direct relation between what you integrate into your text and what you place in parentheses. If, for example, you include an author's name in a sentence, you need not repeat it in the parenthetical page citation that follows. It will be clear that the reference is to the work of the author you have mentioned. The paired sentences below illustrate how to cite authors in the text to keep parenthetical references concise.

**Author's name in text**

`Frye has argued this point before (178-85).`

**Author's name in reference**

`This point has been argued before (Frye 178-85).`

**Authors' names in text**

`Others, like Wellek and Warren (310-15), hold an`

`opposite point of view.`

**Authors' names in reference**

`Others hold an opposite point of view (e.g.,`

`Wellek and Warren 310-15).`

**Author's name in text**

`Only Daiches has seen this relation (2: 776-77).`

**Author's name in reference**

`Only one critic has seen this relation (Daiches 2:`

`776-77).`

**Author's name in text**

It may be true, as Robertson writes, that "in the appreciation of medieval art the attitude of the observer is of primary importance . . ." (136).

**Author's name in reference**

It may be true that "in the appreciation of medieval art the attitude of the observer is of primary importance . . ." (Robertson 136).

To avoid interrupting the flow of your writing, place the parenthetical reference where a pause would naturally occur (preferably at the end of a sentence), as near as possible to the material it documents. The parenthetical reference precedes the punctuation mark that concludes the sentence, clause, or phrase containing the borrowed material.

In his **Autobiography**, Benjamin Franklin states that he prepared a list of thirteen virtues (135-37).

If a quotation comes at the end of the sentence, insert the parenthetical reference between the closing quotation mark and the concluding punctuation mark.

Ernst Rose writes, "The highly spiritual view of the world presented in **Siddartha** exercised its appeal on West and East alike" (74). *— end with punctuation to fit your own sentence. not pune. in quote*

If the quotation is set off from the text (see 2.6.2–3), skip two spaces after the concluding punctuation mark of the quotation and insert the parenthetical reference.

John K. Mahon offers this interesting comment on the War of 1812:

> Financing the war was very difficult at
> the time. Baring Brothers, a banking
> firm of the enemy country, handled
> routine accounts for the United States
> overseas, but the firm would take on no
> loans. The loans were in the end
> absorbed by wealthy Americans at great
> hazard--also, as it turned out, at great
> profit to them. (385)

If you need to document several sources for a statement, you may cite them in a note to avoid unduly disrupting the text (see 5.6).

## 5.5. Sample references

Each of the following sections concludes with a list of the works it cites. Note that the lists for the first five sections (5.5.1–5) do not include more than one work by the same author. On citing two or more works by an author, see 5.5.6.

### 5.5.1. Citing an entire work

If you wish to cite an entire work, rather than part of the work, it is usually preferable to include the author's name in the text rather than in a parenthetical reference.

But Judith Kauffman has offered another view.

The Gunn anthology <u>Literature and Religion</u>
includes many examples of this influence.

Kurosawa's <u>Rashomon</u> was one of the first Japanese
films to attract a Western audience.

John Ciardi's remarks drew warm applause.

I vividly recall the Caldwell production of <u>La</u>
<u>Traviata</u>.

Pattis's introduction to computer programming has
received widespread praise.

Gilbert and Gubar broke new ground on the subject.

Edens et al. have a useful collection of essays on
teaching Shakespeare.

If, however, you choose not to use the author's name in the text, include
it in a parenthetical reference. When citing an entire work, you usually
need only the last name of the author (or editor, translator, speaker,
creative artist, etc.—whichever name you have chosen to begin the entry in the list of works cited). If two or three names begin the entry, give
the last name of each person listed. If one name followed by "et al."

begins the entry, give the last name of the person listed, followed by "et al.," without any intervening punctuation (Edens et al.). Omit other abbreviations, such as ed., trans., comp.: "There is only one introductory book of essays in this field (Gunn)." (See 5.5.4 for works listed by title.)

## Works Cited

Caldwell, Sarah, dir. and cond. <u>La Traviata</u>. By
    Giuseppe Verdi. With Beverly Sills. Opera
    Co. of Boston. Orpheum Theatre, Boston. 4
    Nov. 1972.

Ciardi, John. Address. Opening General Sess.
    NCTE Convention, Washington. 19 Nov. 1982.

Edens, Walter, et al., eds. <u>Teaching</u>
    <u>Shakespeare</u>. Princeton: Princeton UP, 1977.

Gilbert, Sandra M., and Susan Gubar. <u>The Madwoman</u>
    <u>in the Attic: The Woman Writer and the</u>
    <u>Nineteenth-Century Literary Imagination</u>. New
    Haven: Yale UP, 1979.

Gunn, Giles, ed. <u>Literature and Religion</u>. New
    York: Harper, 1971.

Kauffman, Judith. "Musique et matière romanesque
    dans <u>Moderato cantabile</u> de Marguerite
    Duras." <u>Etudes littéraires</u> 15 (1982):
    97-112.

Kurosawa, Akira, dir. <u>Rashomon</u>. With Toshiro

    Mifune and Michiko Kyo. Daiei, 1950.

Pattis, Richard E. <u>Karel the Robot: A Gentle</u>

    <u>Introduction to the Art of Programming</u>.

    Computer software. Cybertronics, 1981.

## 5.5.2. Citing part of an article or of a single-volume book

If you quote, paraphrase, or otherwise use a specific passage in a book or article, give the relevant page numbers. If the author's name is in the text, only the page reference need appear in parentheses. If the context does not clearly identify the author, add the author's last name before the page reference. Leave a space between them, but do not insert punctuation, the word "page(s)," or an abbreviation.

Clark raised some interesting questions concerning

artistic "masterpieces" (1-5, 12-13).


Another particularly appealing passage is the

opening of García Márquez's story "A Very Old Man

with Enormous Wings" (105).


Among intentional spoonerisms, the "punlike

metathesis of distinctive features may serve to

weld together words etymologically unrelated but

close in their sound and meaning" (Jakobson and

Waugh 304).

In Hansberry's <u>A Raisin in the Sun</u> the rejection
of Lindner's tempting offer permits Walter's
family to pursue the new life they had long
dreamed about (274-75).

As Katharina M. Wilson has written, "Intended or
not, the echoes of Tertullian's exhortations in
the <u>Utopia</u> provide yet another level of ambiguity
to More's ironic commentary on social and moral
conditions both in sixteenth-century Europe and in
Nowhere-Land" (73).

A 1983 report found "a decline in the academic
quality of students choosing teaching as a career"
(Hook 10).

## Works Cited

Clark, Kenneth.  <u>What Is a Masterpiece?</u>  London:
     Thames, 1979.

García Márquez, Gabriel.  "A Very Old Man with
     Enormous Wings."  <u>"Leaf Storm" and Other</u>

<u>Stories</u>.  Trans.  Gregory Rabassa.  New York:

Harper, 1972.  105-12.

Hansberry, Lorraine.  <u>A Raisin in the Sun</u>.  <u>Black</u>

<u>Theater: A Twentieth-Century Collection of</u>

<u>the Work of Its Best Playwrights</u>.  Ed.

Lindsay Patterson.  New York: Dodd, 1971.

221-76.

Hook, Janet.  "Raise Standards of Admission,

Colleges Urged."  <u>Chronicle of Higher</u>

<u>Education</u> 4 May 1983: 1+.

Jakobson, Roman, and Linda R. Waugh.  <u>The Sound</u>

<u>Shape of Language</u>.  Bloomington: Indiana UP,

1979.

Wilson, Katharina M.  "Tertullian's <u>De cultu</u>

<u>foeminarum</u> and Utopia."  <u>Moreana</u> 73 (1982):

69-74.

## 5.5.3.  Citing volume and page numbers of a multivolume work

To cite volume numbers as well as page numbers of a multivolume work, give the volume number, a colon, a space, and the page reference: (Wellek 2: 1–10). Use neither the words "volume" and "page" nor abbreviations. It is understood that the number *before* the colon identifies the volume and the number(s) *after* the colon the page(s). If, however, you wish to refer parenthetically to an entire volume of a multivolume work, so that there is no need to cite pages, place a comma after the author's name and include the abbreviation "vol.": (Wellek, vol. 2). If you integrate such a reference into a sentence, spell out "volume" instead of abbreviating it: "In volume 2, Wellek deals with. . . ."

Interest in Afro-American literature in the 1960s
and 1970s inevitably led to "a significant
reassessment of the aesthetic and humanistic
achievements of black writers" (Inge, Duke, and
Bryer 1: v).


Between the years 1945 and 1972, the political
party system in the United States underwent
profound changes (Schlesinger, vol. 4).


Daiches is useful on the Restoration (2: 538-89),
as he is on other periods.


### Works Cited

Daiches, David. <u>A Critical History of English
      Literature</u>. 2nd ed. 2 vols. New York:
      Ronald, 1970.

Inge, M. Thomas, Maurice Duke, and Jackson R.
      Bryer, eds. <u>Black American Writers:</u>
      <u>Bibliographical Essays</u>. 2 vols. New York:

St. Martin's, 1978.

Schlesinger, Arthur M., gen. ed. <u>History of U.S.</u>

　　<u>Political Parties</u>. 4 vols. New York:

　　Chelsea, 1973.

## 5.5.4. Citing a work listed by title

In a parenthetical reference to a work alphabetized by title in the list of works cited, the title (if brief), or a shortened version, replaces the author's name before the page number(s). Omit a page reference, however, if you are citing a one-page article or, of course, a nonprint source. When abbreviating the title of an anonymous work, begin with the word by which it is alphabetized in the list of works cited. It would be a mistake, for example, to cite the book *Glossary of Terms Used in Heraldry* as *Heraldry* since your reader would then look for the bibliographic entry under "H" rather than "G." (See also citing books by corporate authors, 5.5.5.)

The nine grades of mandarins were "distinguished

by the color of the button on the hats of

office . . ." ("Mandarin").

According to the <u>Handbook of Korea</u>, much Korean

sculpture is associated with Buddhism (241-47).

<u>Computerworld</u> has devoted a thoughtful editorial

to the issue of government and technology ("Uneasy

Silence"), and one hopes that such public

discussion will continue in the future.

Later, when the characters are confronted by
tragedy, they take on greater depth ("Joy Ride").


                    Works Cited

A Handbook of Korea. 4th ed. Seoul: Korean

     Overseas Information Service, Ministry of

     Culture and Information, 1982.

"The Joy Ride." Writ. Alfred Shaughnessy.

     Upstairs, Downstairs. Created by Eileen

     Atkins and Jean Marsh. Dir. Bill Bain.

     Prod. John Hawkesworth. Masterpiece

     Theatre. Introd. Alistair Cooke. PBS.

     WGBH, Boston. 6 Feb. 1977.

"Mandarin." Encyclopedia Americana. 1980 ed.

"An Uneasy Silence." Editorial. Computerworld

     28 Mar. 1983: 54.

## 5.5.5. Citing a work by a corporate author

To cite a work listed by a corporate author, you may use the corporate author's name followed by a page reference: (United Nations, Economic Commission for Africa 79–86). It is better, however, to include such a long name in the text to avoid interrupting the reading with an extended parenthetical reference.

In 1963 the United Nations' Economic Commission

for Africa predicted that Africa would evolve into

an industrially advanced economy within fifty

years (1, 4-6).


The Commission on the Humanities has concluded

that "the humanities are inescapably bound to

literacy" (69).


Works Cited

Commission on the Humanities.  The Humanities in

    American Life: Report of the Commission on

    the Humanities.  Berkeley: U of California P,

    1980.

United Nations.  Economic Commission for Africa.

    Industrial Growth in Africa.  New York:

    United Nations, 1963.

## 5.5.6. Citing two or more works by the same author(s)

To cite one of two or more works by the same author(s), put a comma after the last name(s) of the author(s) and add the title of the work (if brief), or a shortened version, and the relevant page reference: (Borroff, *Wallace Stevens* 2), (Durant and Durant, *Age of Voltaire* 214–48). If you state the author's name in the text, give only the title and page reference: (*Wallace Stevens* 2), (*Age of Voltaire* 214–48). If you include both the author's name and the title in the text, indicate only the pertinent page number(s) in parentheses: (2), (214–48).

Borroff finds Stevens "dominated by two powerful

and contending temperamental strains" (<u>Wallace
Stevens</u> 2).

In <u>The Age of Voltaire</u> the Durants portray
eighteenth-century England as "a humble satellite"
in the world of music and art (214-48).

As E. L. Doctorow has written, "The Dreiserian
universe is composed of merchants, workers,
club-men, managers, actors, salesmen, doormen,
cops, derelicts . . ." (Introduction ix).

The <u>Gawain</u> Poet has been called a "master of
juxtaposition" (Borroff, <u>Sir Gawain</u> viii) and has
been praised for other poetic achievements.

To Will and Ariel Durant, creative men and women
make "history forgivable by enriching our heritage
and our lives" (<u>Dual Autobiography</u> 406).

The brief but dramatic conclusion of chapter 13 of

Doctorow's <u>Welcome to Hard Times</u> constitutes the

climax of the novel (209-12).


Works Cited

Borroff, Marie, trans. <u>Sir Gawain and the Green</u>

<u>Knight</u>. New York: Norton, 1967.

---, ed. <u>Wallace Stevens: A Collection of</u>

<u>Critical Essays</u>. Englewood Cliffs: Prentice,

1963.

Doctorow, E. L. Introduction. <u>Sister Carrie</u>. By

Theodore Dreiser. New York: Bantam, 1982.

v-xi.

---. <u>Welcome to Hard Times</u>. 1960. New York:

Bantam, 1976.

Durant, Will, and Ariel Durant. <u>The Age of</u>

<u>Voltaire</u>. Vol. 9 of <u>The Story of</u>

<u>Civilization</u>. New York: Simon, 1965.

---. <u>A Dual Autobiography</u>. New York: Simon,

1977.

## 5.5.7. Citing indirect sources

Whenever you can, take material from the original source, not a sec-
ondhand one. Sometimes, however, the original is not available and the
only source is an indirect one: for example, someone's published ac-

count of another's spoken remarks. If you quote or paraphrase a quotation from another book, put the abbreviation "qtd. in" ("quoted in")
before the indirect source you cite in your parenthetical reference. (You
may document the original source in a note; see 5.6.1.)

Samuel Johnson admitted that Edmund Burke was an

"extraordinary man" (qtd. in Boswell 2: 450).

The remarks of Bernardo Segni and Lionardo

Salviati demonstrate that they were not faithful

disciples of Aristotle (qtd. in Weinberg 1: 405,

616-17).

### Works Cited

Boswell, James. <u>The Life of Johnson</u>.  Ed. George

    Birkbeck Hill and L. F. Powell.  6 vols.

    Oxford: Clarendon, 1934-50.

Weinberg, Bernard.  <u>A History of Literary

    Criticism in the Italian Renaissance</u>.  2

    vols.  Chicago: U of Chicago P, 1961.

## 5.5.8.  Citing literary works

In references to classic prose works available in several editions (e.g.,
novels and plays), it is helpful to provide more information than just the
page number of the edition used; a chapter number, for example, would
enable readers to locate a quotation in any copy of the novel. In such
references, give the page number first, add a semicolon, and then give

other identifying information, using appropriate abbreviations—for example, (130; ch. 9), (271; bk. 4, ch. 2).

When we first encounter Raskolnikov in <u>Crime and Punishment</u>, Dostoevsky presents us with a man contemplating a terrible act but terrified of meeting his talkative landlady on the stairs (1; pt. 1, ch. 1).

Mary Wollstonecraft recollects in <u>A Vindication of the Rights of Woman</u> many "women who, not led by degrees to proper studies, and not permitted to choose for themselves, have indeed been overgrown children . . ." (185; ch. 13, sec. 2).

In one version of the story, William Tell's son urges his reluctant father to shoot the arrow (Sastre 315; sc. 6).

In citing classic verse plays and poems, omit page numbers altogether and cite by division(s) (e.g., canto, book, part, act, or scene) and line(s), with periods separating the various numbers—for example, *Iliad* 9.19 refers to book 9, line 19, of Homer's *Iliad*. Never use the abbreviations "l." or "ll.," which can be confused with numerals, in references to poetic works. Instead, if you are citing only line numbers, initially use the word "line" or "lines" and, once you have established that the numbers designate lines, use the numbers alone.

In general, use arabic numerals rather than roman numerals in citing division and page numbers. But always use roman numerals, of course,

when citing pages that are so numbered (e.g., a preface). In addition,
some prefer roman numerals for citing acts and scenes in plays (e.g.,
*King Lear* IV.i). If your instructor does not recommend this practice,
however, use arabic numerals: *King Lear* 4.1. (On numbers, see 2.4.)

When included in parenthetical references, the titles of the books of
the Bible and of famous literary works are often abbreviated—for example, 1 Chron. 21.8, Rev. 21.3, *Oth.* 4.2.7–13, *FQ* 3.3.53.3. The most
widely used and accepted abbreviations for such titles are listed in 6.7.
Follow prevailing practices, as indicated by your sources, for other abbreviations (*Troilus* for Chaucer's *Troilus and Criseyde*, *OF* for Arios-
to's *Orlando Furioso*, *PL* for Milton's *Paradise Lost*, "Nightingale" for
Keats's "Ode to a Nightingale," etc.). In the following example the reference is to lines 1791 and 1792 of book 5 of Chaucer's *Troilus and Criseyde.*

Chaucer urges one of his "litel boks" to kiss "the

steppes, where as thow seest pace / Virgile,

Ovide, Omer, Lucan, and Stace" (<u>Troilus</u>

5.1791-92), using a figure much imitated by later

English poets.

Works Cited

Chaucer, Geoffrey.  <u>The Works of Geoffrey</u>

<u>Chaucer</u>.  Ed. F. N. Robinson.  2nd ed.

Boston: Houghton, 1957.

Dostoevsky, Feodor.  <u>Crime and Punishment</u>.  Trans.

Jessie Coulson.  Ed. George Gibian.  New

York: Norton, 1964.

Sastre, Alfonso.  <u>Sad Are the Eyes of William</u>

<u>Tell</u>.  Trans. Leonard Pronko.  <u>The New Wave</u>

<u>Spanish Drama</u>.  Ed. George Wellwarth.  New

York: New York UP, 1970.  165-321.

Wollstonecraft, Mary.  <u>A Vindication of the Rights</u>

<u>of Woman</u>.  Ed. Carol H. Poston.  New York:

Norton, 1975.

## 5.5.9. Citing more than one work in a single parenthetical reference

If you wish to include two or more works in a single parenthetical reference, cite each work as you normally would in a reference, but use semicolons to separate the citations.

(Frye 42; Brée 101-33)

(National Committee 25-35; Brody C5)

(Potter et al., vol. 1; Boyle 96-125)

(Booth, "Kenneth Burke's" 22; Cassirer 1: 295-319)

(Wellek and Warren; Booth, <u>Critical Understanding</u>

45-52)

(Blocker, Plummer, and Richardson 52-57; Carnegie

Council 15)

Keep in mind, however, that long parenthetical references—for example, (Stratman; Potter et al. 1: 176-202; Bondanella and Bondanella, "Lauda"; Curley ii-vii; Rey-Flaud 37-43, 187-201; Pikeryng A2r)—may prove intrusive and disconcerting to the reader. To avoid an excessive disruption, cite multiple sources in a note rather than in parentheses in the text (see 5.6.2).


## Works Cited

Blocker, Clyde E., Robert H. Plummer, and Richard

 C. Richardson, Jr. <u>The Two-Year College: A</u>

 <u>Social Synthesis</u>. Englewood Cliffs:

 Prentice, 1965.

Bondanella, Peter, and Julia Conaway Bondanella,

 eds. <u>Dictionary of Italian Literature</u>.

 Westport: Greenwood, 1979.

Booth, Wayne C. <u>Critical Understanding: The</u>

 <u>Powers and Limits of Pluralism</u>. Chicago: U

 of Chicago P, 1979.

---. "Kenneth Burke's Way of Knowing." <u>Critical</u>

 <u>Inquiry</u> 1 (1974): 1-22.

Boyle, Anthony T. "The Epistemological Evolution

 of Renaissance Utopian Literature:

 1516-1657." Diss. New York U, 1983.

Brée, Germaine. <u>Women Writers in France:</u>

 <u>Variations on a Theme</u>. New Brunswick:

 Rutgers UP, 1973.

Brody, Jane.  "Heart Attacks: Turmoil beneath the

Calm."  New York Times 21 June 1983, late

ed.: C1+.

Carnegie Council on Policy Studies in Higher

Education.  Giving Youth a Better Chance:

Options for Education, Work, and Service.

San Francisco: Jossey, 1980.

Cassirer, Ernst.  The Philosophy of Symbolic

Forms.  Trans. Ralph Manheim.  3 vols.  New

Haven: Yale UP, 1955.

Curley, Michael, trans.  Physiologus.  Austin: U

of Texas P, 1979.

Frye, Northrop.  Anatomy of Criticism: Four

Essays.  Princeton: Princeton UP, 1957.

National Committee on Careers for Older

Americans.  Older Americans: An Untapped

Resource.  Washington: Acad. for Educ. Dev.,

1979.

Pikeryng, John.  A Newe Enterlude of Vice

Conteyninge the Historye of Horestes.

London, 1567.

Potter, G. R., et al. <u>The New Cambridge Modern</u>

    <u>History</u>. 14 vols. Cambridge: Cambridge UP,

    1957-70.

Rey-Flaud, Henri. <u>Pour une dramaturgie du Moyen</u>

    <u>Age</u>. Paris: PUF, 1980.

Stratman, Carl J., comp. and ed. <u>Bibliography of</u>

    <u>English Printed Tragedy, 1565-1900</u>.

    Carbondale: Southern Illinois UP, 1966.

Wellek, René, and Austin Warren. <u>Theory of</u>

    <u>Literature</u>. 3rd ed. New York: Harcourt,

    1962.

## 5.6. Using notes with parenthetical documentation

The following types of notes may be used with parenthetical documentation:

1. Content notes offering the reader comment, explanation, or information that the text cannot accommodate

2. Bibliographic notes containing either several sources or evaluative comments on sources

In providing this sort of supplementary information, place a superscript arabic numeral at the appropriate place in the text (see 5.8.2) and write the note after a matching numeral either at the end of the text (an endnote) or at the bottom of the page (a footnote) (see 5.8.4).

### 5.6.1. Content notes

Avoid essaylike notes, which divert the reader's attention from the primary text. In general, if you cannot fit comments into the text, omit them unless they are essential to justify or clarify what you have written. You may use a note, for example, to give full publication facts for an original source for which you cite an indirect source and perhaps to explain why you worked from secondary material.

The remarks of Bernardo Segni and Lionardo Salviati demonstrate that they were not faithful disciples of Aristotle.[1]


### Note

[1] Bernardo Segni, <u>Rettorica et poetica d'Aristotile</u> (Florence, 1549), 281, qtd. in Weinberg 1: 405; Lionardo Salviati, <u>Poetica d'Aristotile parafrasata e comentata</u> (Florence, 1586), ms. 2.2.11, Bibl. Naz. Centrale, Florence, 140v, qtd. in Weinberg 1: 616-17.

For more information on using notes for documentation purposes, see 5.8.

### Work Cited

Weinberg, Bernard. <u>A History of Literary Criticism in the Italian Renaissance</u>. 2 vols. Chicago: U of Chicago P, 1961.

## 5.6.2. Bibliographic notes

Use notes for evaluative comments on sources and for references containing numerous citations.

For older people, the past decade has represented the best of times and the worst of times.[1]

It is a difficult task to attempt to chart the
development of drama in the context of medieval
and Renaissance Europe.[2]

### Notes

[1] For contrasting points of view, see
National Committee and Brody C5.

[2] For a sampling of useful source
materials, see Potter et al. 1: 176-202;
Bondanella and Bondanella, "Lauda"; Rey-Flaud
37-43, 187-201; and Stratman.

### Works Cited

Bondanella, Peter, and Julia Conaway Bondanella,
    eds. <u>Dictionary of Italian Literature</u>.
    Westport: Greenwood, 1979.

Brody, Jane. "Heart Attacks: Turmoil beneath the
    Calm." <u>New York Times</u> 21 June 1983, late
    ed.: C1+.

National Committee on Careers for Older
    Americans. <u>Older Americans: An Untapped</u>

<u>Resource</u>.  Washington: Acad. for Educ. Dev.,

  1979.

Potter, G. R., et al.  <u>The New Cambridge Modern</u>

  <u>History</u>.  14 vols.  Cambridge: Cambridge UP,

  1957-70.

Rey-Flaud, Henri.  <u>Pour une dramaturgie du Moyen</u>

  <u>Age</u>.  Paris: PUF, 1980.

Stratman, Carl J., comp. and ed.  <u>Bibliography of</u>

  <u>English Printed Tragedy, 1565-1900</u>.

  Carbondale: Southern Illinois UP, 1966.

# 5.7.  Other types of parenthetical documentation

Other types of parenthetical documentation include: (1) the author-date system, (2) the number system, and (3) the placement of full publication information in the text.

## 5.7.1.  Author-date system

The author-date system, the most common in the social and physical sciences, requires that a parenthetical reference include the author's last name and the year of publication (unless given in the text), followed by a comma and the page reference: (Wilson 1982, 73). Information cited in the text is omitted from the parenthetical reference.

This system also requires a slight change in bibliographic form: to assist the reader in finding the appropriate entry in the list of works cited, the year of publication immediately follows the author's name. The title of the work and the remaining publication information complete the entry. If the list includes more than one work by an author, the entries are arranged chronologically. If two or more works by the same author were published in a given year, each is assigned a lowercase letter: 1979a, 1979b.

In <u>The Age of Voltaire</u> the Durants portray
eighteenth-century England as a "humble satellite"
in the world of music and art (1965, 214-48).

The <u>alazon</u> is a "self-deceiving or self-deceived
character in fiction" (Frye 1957a, 365).

Daiches is useful on the Restoration (1970, 2:
538-89), as he is on other periods.

As Katharina M. Wilson has written, "Intended or
not, the echoes of Tertullian's exhortations in
the <u>Utopia</u> provide yet another level of ambiguity
to More's ironic commentary on social and moral
conditions both in sixteenth-century Europe and in
Nowhere-Land" (1982, 73).

There are several excellent essays in the volume
<u>Sound and Poetry</u> (Frye 1957b).

To Will and Ariel Durant, creative men and women

make "history forgivable by enriching our heritage
and our lives" (1977, 406).


### Works Cited

Daiches, David.  1970.  <u>A Critical History of
English Literature</u>.  2nd ed.  2 vols.  New
York: Ronald.

Durant, Will, and Ariel Durant.  1965.  <u>The Age of
Voltaire</u>.  Vol. 9 of <u>The Story of
Civilization</u>.  New York: Simon.

---.  1977.  <u>A Dual Autobiography</u>.  New York:
Simon.

Frye, Northrop.  1957a.  <u>Anatomy of Criticism:
Four Essays</u>.  Princeton: Princeton UP.

---, ed.  1957b.  <u>Sound and Poetry</u>.  New York:
Columbia UP.

Wilson, Katharina M.  1982.  "Tertullian's <u>De
cultu foeminarum</u> and Utopia."  <u>Moreana</u> 73:
69-74.

## 5.7.2.  Number system

In the number system, arabic numerals designate entries in the list of
works cited and appear in parenthetical documentation (sometimes underlined) along with the relevant page reference, which follows a com-

ma. With this system, the year of publication remains at the end of the bibliographic entry. In the number system, the works cited may be listed in any useful order. (In the sciences, for example, they are frequently listed in the order in which they are first cited in the text.)


The <u>alazon</u> is a "self-deceiving or self-deceived character in fiction" (<u>2</u>, 365).


In <u>The Age of Voltaire</u> the Durants portray eighteenth-century England as a "humble satellite" in the world of music and art (<u>1</u>, 214-48).


There are several excellent essays in the volume <u>Sound and Poetry</u> (<u>3</u>).


Works Cited

1. Durant, Will, and Ariel Durant.  <u>The Age of Voltaire</u>.  Vol. 9 of <u>The Story of Civilization</u>.  New York: Simon, 1965.

2. Frye, Northrop.  <u>Anatomy of Criticism: Four Essays</u>.  Princeton: Princeton UP, 1957.

3. ---, ed.  <u>Sound and Poetry</u>.  New York: Columbia UP, 1957.

### 5.7.3. Full publication information in parenthetical references

The practice of placing full publication information in parenthetical references is seldom followed because it deprives the reader of the benefits of a list of works cited and interrupts the flow of the text. Sometimes, however, it is adopted in bibliographic studies or in works requiring few references. As in other systems, information given in the text is not repeated in the reference. Square brackets are used for parentheses within parentheses.

The alazon, as Northrop Frye describes it, is a

"self-deceiving or self-deceived character in

fiction" (Anatomy of Criticism: Four Essays

[Princeton: Princeton UP, 1957] 365).

In his A Critical History of English Literature

David Daiches is useful on the Restoration (2nd

ed., 2 vols. [New York: Ronald, 1970] 2: 538-89),

as he is on other periods.

## 5.8. Using notes for documentation

Another system of documentation entails using endnotes or footnotes to cite sources.

### 5.8.1. Documentation notes versus the list of works cited and parenthetical references

When notes are used for documentation, a list of works cited or a bibliography may not be required. (Check your instructor's preference.) First note references include the publication information found in a bibliographic entry—the author's name, the title, and the publication facts—as well as the specific page reference. (Subsequent references to a work require less information; see 5.8.8.) Note form, however, differs slightly from bibliographic form (see 5.8.3), and note numbers replace parenthetical references at appropriate points in the text to draw the reader's attention to citations (see 5.8.2). Documentation notes appear either at the end of the text, as endnotes, or at the bottoms of relevant pages, as footnotes (see 5.8.4).

## 5.8.2.  Note numbers

Notes are numbered consecutively, starting from 1, throughout a research paper, except for any notes accompanying special material, such as a figure or a table (see 3.7). They are not numbered by individual pages or indicated by asterisks or other symbols. Note numbers are "superior" or "superscript" figures—arabic numerals typed slightly above the line, like this,[1] without periods, parentheses, or slashes. They follow punctuation marks except dashes. In general, to avoid interrupting the continuity of the text, note numbers, like parenthetical references, are placed at the end of the sentence, clause, or phrase containing the material quoted or referred to.

## 5.8.3.  Note form versus bibliographic form

With some exceptions, documentary notes and bibliographic entries provide the same information but differ in form.

### Bibliographic form

A bibliographic entry has three main divisions, each followed by a period: the author's name reversed for alphabetizing, the title, and the publishing data.

```
Frye, Northrop.  Anatomy of Criticism: Four

     Essays.  Princeton: Princeton UP, 1957.
```

### Note form

A documentary note has four main divisions, with a period only at the end: the author's name in normal order, followed by a comma; the title; the publishing data in parentheses; and a page reference.

```
1 Northrop Frye, Anatomy of Criticism: Four

Essays (Princeton: Princeton UP, 1957) 52.
```

## 5.8.4.  Endnotes and footnotes

In research papers, make all notes endnotes, unless you are instructed otherwise. As their name implies, endnotes appear after the text, starting on a new page numbered in sequence with the preceding page. Type the title "Notes" centered and one inch from the top, double-space, indent five spaces from the left margin, and type the note number, without punctuation, slightly above the line. Leave a space and type the reference. If the note extends to two or more lines, begin subsequent lines at the left margin. Type the notes consecutively, double-spaced, and number all pages.

Footnotes appear at the bottoms of pages, beginning four lines (two double spaces) below the text. Single-space footnotes but double-space between them. When a note continues on the following page, type a solid line across the new page one line (one double space) below the last line of the text and continue the note four lines (a total of two double spaces) below the text. Footnotes for the new page immediately follow the note continued from the previous page.

## 5.8.5.  Sample first note references: Books

Bibliographic entries corresponding to the following sample notes appear in the sections indicated in parentheses after the headings. Consult the appropriate section if you need additional information on citing a particular type of reference.

**a.  A book by a single author (4.5.1)**

> [1] Frank McConnell, <u>Storytelling and</u>
>
> <u>Mythmaking: Images from Film and Literature</u> (New
>
> York: Oxford UP, 1979) 32.

**b.  An anthology or compilation (4.5.2)**

> [2] Fred J. Nichols, ed. and trans., <u>An</u>
>
> <u>Anthology of Neo-Latin Poetry</u> (New Haven: Yale UP,
>
> 1979) vii-viii.

**c.  A book by multiple authors (4.5.4)**

> [3] Clyde E. Blocker, Robert H. Plummer, and
>
> Richard C. Richardson, Jr., <u>The Two-Year College:</u>

A Social Synthesis (Englewood Cliffs: Prentice,

1965) 52-57.

d.  A book by a corporate author (4.5.6)

4 Commission on the Humanities, The

Humanities in American Life: Report of the

Commission on the Humanities (Berkeley: U of

California P, 1980) 69.

e.  An anonymous book (4.5.7)

5 A Handbook of Korea, 4th ed. (Seoul:

Korean Overseas Information Service, Ministry of

Culture and Information, 1982) 241-47.

f.  A work in an anthology (4.5.8)

6 Gabriel García Márquez, "A Very Old Man

with Enormous Wings," "Leaf Storm" and Other

Stories, trans. Gregory Rabassa (New York: Harper,

1972) 105.

7 Lorraine Hansberry, A Raisin in the Sun,

Black Theater: A Twentieth-Century Collection of

the Work of Its Best Playwrights, ed. Lindsay

Patterson (New York: Dodd, 1971) 265-76.

g.  An introduction, preface, foreword, or afterword (4.5.9)

8 Edgar Johnson, afterword, <u>David</u> <u>Copperfield</u>, by Charles Dickens (New York: Signet-NAL, 1962) 875.

h.  A multivolume work (4.5.11)

9 David Daiches, <u>A Critical History of</u> <u>English Literature</u>, 2nd ed., 2 vols. (New York: Ronald, 1970) 2: 538-39.

10 Arthur M. Schlesinger, gen. ed., <u>History</u> <u>of U.S. Political Parties</u>, 4 vols. (New York: Chelsea, 1973) vol. 4.

i.  An "edition" (4.5.12)

11 Geoffrey Chaucer, <u>The Works of Geoffrey</u> <u>Chaucer</u>, ed. F. N. Robinson, 2nd ed. (Boston: Houghton, 1957) 545.

12 Jo Ann Boydston, ed., <u>Psychology</u>, by John Dewey, vol. 2 of <u>John Dewey: The Early Works,</u> <u>1882-1898</u> (Carbondale: Southern Illinois UP, 1967) 85-87.

j.  A translation (4.5.13)

13 Feodor Dostoevsky, <u>Crime and Punishment</u>,

trans. Jessie Coulson, ed. George Gibian (New
York: Norton, 1964) 157.

[14] Joseph G. Fucilla, trans., <u>Three
Melodramas</u>, by Pietro Metastasio, Studies in
Romance Langs. 24 (Lexington: UP of Kentucky,
1981) 1-14.

k.  A republished book (4.5.14)

[15] E. L. Doctorow, <u>Welcome to Hard Times</u>
(1960; New York: Bantam, 1976) 209-12.

l.  An article in a reference book (4.5.15)

[16] "Mandarin," <u>Encyclopedia Americana</u>, 1980
ed.

m.  A pamphlet (4.5.16)

[17] <u>Capital Punishment: Cruel and Unusual?</u>
(Plano: Instructional Aides, 1982) 11-21.

n.  Government publications (4.5.17)

[18] United Nations, Economic Commission for
Africa, <u>Industrial Growth in Africa</u> (New York:
United Nations, 1963) 4-6.

o.  A book in a series (4.5.18)

[19] Arnold P. Hinchcliffe, <u>Harold Pinter</u>,

rev. ed., Twayne's English Authors Series 51
(Boston: Twayne, 1981) 62.

p.  A publisher's imprint (4.5.19)

[20] Terry Brooks, <u>The Elfstones of Shannara</u>
(New York: Del Rey-Ballantine, 1982) 206.

q.  Multiple publishers (4.5.20)

[21] J. Wight Duff, <u>A Literary History of
Rome: From the Origins to the Close of the Golden
Age</u>, ed. A. M. Duff, 3rd ed. (London: Benn; New
York: Barnes, 1967) 88.

r.  Published proceedings of a conference (4.5.21)

[22] Alan M. Gordon and Evelyn Rugg, eds.,
<u>Actas del Sexto Congreso Internacional de
Hispanistas celebrado en Toronto del 22 al 26
agosto 1977</u> (Toronto: Dept. of Spanish and
Portuguese, U of Toronto, 1980) v-vii.

s.  A book in a language other than English (4.5.22)

[23] Barbara Wachowicz, <u>Marie jeho života</u>
(Praha [Prague]: Lidové, 1979) 1-15.

t.  A book with a title within its title (4.5.23)

[24] Leonard Mades, <u>The Armor and the

Brocade: A Study of Don Quijote and The Courtier

(New York: Las Americas, 1968) 5-11.

**u. A book published before 1900 (4.5.24)**

25 John Dewey, The Study of Ethics: A

Syllabus (Ann Arbor, 1894) 104.

**v. A book without place of publication, publisher, date of publication, or pagination (4.5.25)**

26 Zvi Malachi, ed., Proceedings of the

International Conference on Literary and

Linguistic Computing ([Tel Aviv]: [Tel Aviv U Fac.

of Humanities], n.d.) 1-3.

**w. An unpublished dissertation (4.5.26)**

27 Nancy Kay Johnson, "Cultural and

Psychosocial Determinants of Health and Illness,"

diss., U of Washington, 1980, 34.

**x. A published dissertation (4.5.27)**

28 Rudolf E. Dietze, Ralph Ellison: The

Genesis of an Artist, diss., U Erlangen-Nürnberg,

1982, Erlanger Beiträge zur Sprach- und

Kunstwissenschaft 70 (Nürnberg: Carl, 1982) 168.

## 5.8.6. Sample first note references: Articles in periodicals

For additional information on citing the following types of sources, consult the related sections for bibliographic entries, indicated in parentheses after the headings.

**a. An article in a journal with continuous pagination (4.7.1)**

[1] Karen Spear, "Building Cognitive Skills in Basic Writers," Teaching English in the Two-Year College 9 (1983): 94.

*volume no.*

**b. An article in a journal that pages each issue separately or that uses only issue numbers (4.7.2)**

[2] Frederick Barthelme, "Architecture," Kansas Quarterly 13.3-4 (1981): 77-78.

[3] Allan Pritchard, "West of the Great Divide: A View of the Literature of British Columbia," Canadian Literature 94 (1982): 100-01.

**c. An article from a journal with more than one series (4.7.3)**

[4] Robert Avery, "Foreign Influence on the Nautical Terminology of Russian in the Eighteenth Century," Oxford Slavonic Papers ns 14 (1981): 83.

[5] Michael P. Johnson, "Runaway Slaves and the Slave Communities in South Carolina, 1799-1830," William and Mary Quarterly 3rd ser. 38 (1981): 438-41.

**d. An article from a weekly or biweekly periodical (4.7.4)**

   6 Kim McDonald, "Space Shuttle <u>Columbia</u>'s

Weightless Laboratory Attracts Research,"

<u>Chronicle of Higher Education</u> 28 Oct. 1981: 6.

**e. An article from a monthly or bimonthly periodical (4.7.5)**

   7 Mark Snyder, "Self-Fulfilling

Stereotypes," <u>Psychology Today</u> July 1982: 68.

**f. An article from a daily newspaper (4.7.6)**

   8 Jane Brody, "Heart Attacks: Turmoil

beneath the Calm," <u>New York Times</u> 21 June 1983,

late ed.: C1.

**g. An editorial (4.7.7)**

   9 Morton Malkofsky, "Let the Unions

Negotiate What's Negotiable," editorial, <u>Learning</u>

Oct. 1982: 6.

**h. An anonymous article (4.7.8)**

   10 "Portents for Future Learning," <u>Time</u> 21

Sept. 1981: 65.

**i. A letter to the editor (4.7.9)**

   11 Harry Levin, letter, <u>Partisan Review</u> 47

(1980): 320.

**j.  A review (4.7.10)**

 12 John Updike, "Cohn's Doom," rev. of

God's Grace, by Bernard Malamud, New Yorker 8 Nov.

1982: 169.

 13 Sherley Ashton, rev. of Death and Dying,

by David L. Bender and Richard C. Hagen, Humanist

July-Aug. 1982: 60.

 14 "The Cooling of an Admiration," rev. of

Pound/Joyce: The Letters of Ezra Pound to James

Joyce, ed. Forrest Read, Times Literary Supplement

6 Mar. 1969: 239-40.

 15 Rev. of Anthology of Danish Literature,

ed. F. J. Billeskov Jansen and P. M. Mitchell,

Times Literary Supplement 7 July 1972: 785.

**k.  An article whose title contains a quotation or a title
within quotation marks (4.7.11)**

 16 E. E. Duncan-Jones, "Moore's 'A Kiss à

l'Antique' and Keats's 'Ode on a Grecian Urn,'"

Notes and Queries ns 28 (1981): 316-17.

**l.  An abstract from *Dissertation Abstracts* or *Dissertation
Abstracts International* (4.7.12)**

 17 Nancy Kay Johnson, "Cultural and

Psychosocial Determinants of Health and Illness,"

<u>DAI</u> 40 (1980): 4235B (U of Washington).

## 5.8.7.  Sample first references: Other sources

For additional information on the following types of documentation, consult the related sections for bibliographic entries, indicated in parentheses after the headings.

**a.  Computer software (4.8.1)**

[1] <u>Connections</u>, computer software, Krell

Software, 1982.

[2] Richard E. Pattis, <u>Karel the Robot: A</u>

<u>Gentle Introduction to the Art of Programming</u>,

computer software, Cybertronics, 1981.

**b.  Material from a computer service (4.8.2)**

[3] Howard Schomer, "South Africa: Beyond

Fair Employment," <u>Harvard Business Review</u> May–June

1983: 145+ (DIALOG file 122, item 119425 833160).

[4] "Barbara Bush Turner," <u>American Men and</u>

<u>Women of Science</u>, 15th ed. (Bowker, 1983) (DIALOG

file 236, item 0107406).

**c.  Material from an information service (4.8.3)**

[5] Bernard Spolsky, <u>Navajo Language</u>

<u>Maintenance: Six-Year-Olds in 1969</u>, Navajo Reading

Study Prog. Rept. 5 (Albuquerque: U of New Mexico,

1969) 22 (ERIC ED 043 044).

6 Paul R. Streiff, <u>Some Criteria for</u>
<u>Designing Evaluation of TESOL Programs</u> (ERIC,
1970) 10 (ED 040 385).

**d. Radio and television programs (4.8.4)**

7 "The Joy Ride," writ. Alfred Shaughnessy,
<u>Upstairs, Downstairs</u>, created by Eileen Atkins and
Jean Marsh, dir. Bill Bain, prod. John
Hawkesworth, Masterpiece Theatre, introd. Alistair
Cooke, PBS, WGBH, Boston, 6 Feb. 1977.

**e. Recordings (4.8.5)**

8 Wolfgang A. Mozart, Symphony no. 35 in D
and Overtures to <u>The Marriage of Figaro</u>, <u>The Magic</u>
<u>Flute</u>, and <u>Don Giovanni</u>, cond. Antonia Brico,
Mostly Mozart Orch., Columbia, M33888, 1976.

9 Robert Frost, "The Road Not Taken,"
<u>Robert Frost Reads His Poetry</u>, Caedmon, TC 1060,
1956.

10 D. K. Wilgus, Southern Folk Tales,
audiotape, rec. 23-25 Mar. 1965, U of California,
Los Angeles, Archives of Folklore, B.76.82 (7 1/2
ips, 7" reel).

[11] David Lewiston, jacket notes, <u>The</u>
<u>Balinese Gamelan: Music from the Morning of the</u>
<u>World</u>, Nonesuch Explorer Series, H-2015, n.d.

f.  Films, filmstrips, slide programs, videotapes (4.8.6)

[12] <u>Det Sjunde Inseglet</u> [<u>The Seventh Seal</u>],
dir. Ingmar Bergman, Svensk Filmindustri, 1956.

[13] <u>Consumer Awareness: Supply, Demand,</u>
<u>Competition, and Prices</u>, sound filmstrip, prod.
Visual Education, Maclean Hunter Learning
Resources, 1981 (85 fr., 11 min.).

g.  Performances (4.8.7)

[14] George Balanchine, chor., <u>Mozartiana</u>,
with Suzanne Farrell, New York City Ballet, New
York State Theater, 20 Nov. 1981.

[15] Scott Joplin, <u>Treemonisha</u>, dir. Frank
Corsaro, cond. Gunther Schuller, with Carmen
Balthrop, Betty Allen, and Curtis Rayam, Houston
Grand Opera, Miller Theatre, Houston, 18 May 1975.

h.  Musical compositions (4.8.8)

[16] Ludwig van Beethoven, Symphony no. 7 in
A, op. 92.

i. **Works of art (4.8.9)**

17 Rembrandt van Rijn, <u>Aristotle</u>
<u>Contemplating the Bust of Homer</u>, Metropolitan
Museum of Art, New York.

18 Mary Cassatt, <u>Mother and Child</u>, Wichita
Art Museum, Wichita, slide 22 of <u>American</u>
<u>Painting: 1560-1913</u>, by John Pearce (New York:
McGraw, 1964).

j. **Letters (4.8.10)**

19 William Makepeace Thackeray, "To George
Henry Lewes," 6 Mar. 1848, letter 452 of <u>Letters</u>
<u>and Private Papers of William Makepeace Thackeray</u>,
ed. Gordon N. Ray, 4 vols. (Cambridge: Harvard UP,
1946) 2: 353-54.

20 Thomas Hart Benton, letter to John
Charles Fremont, 22 June 1847, John Charles
Fremont Papers, Southwest Museum Library, Los
Angeles.

21 Aaron Copland, letter to the author, 17
May 1982.

k. **Interviews (4.8.11)**

22 Federico Fellini, "The Long Interview,"

_Juliet of the Spirits_, ed. Tullio Kezich, trans.

Howard Greenfield (New York: Ballantine, 1966) 56.

[23] Suzanne Gordon, interview, _All Things_

_Considered_, Natl. Public Radio, WNYC, New York, 1

June 1983.

[24] I. M. Pei, personal interview, 27 July

1983.

l. Maps and charts (4.8.12)

[25] _Canada_, map (Chicago: Rand, 1983).

[26] _Grammar and Punctuation_, chart (Grand

Haven: School Zone, 1980).

m. Cartoons (4.8.13)

[27] Charles Schulz, "Peanuts," cartoon,

_Star-Ledger_ [Newark, NJ] 4 Sept. 1980: 72.

[28] Charles Addams, cartoon, _New Yorker_ 21

Feb. 1983: 41.

n. Lectures, speeches, addresses (4.8.14)

[29] Florence Ridley, "Forget the Past,

Reject the Future: Chaos Is Come Again," Div. on

Teaching of Literature, MLA Convention, Los

Angeles, 28 Dec. 1982.

30 John Ciardi, address, Opening General

Sess., NCTE Convention, Washington, 19 Nov. 1982.

o.  **Manuscripts and typescripts (4.8.15)**

31 Mark Twain, Notebook 32, ts., Mark Twain

Papers, U of California, Berkeley, 50.

p.  **Legal references (4.8.16)**

32 Stevens v. National Broadcasting Co.,

148 USPQ 755 (Calif. Super. Ct. 1966).

## 5.8.8.  Subsequent references

After full documentation has been given for a work, a shortened form is used in subsequent notes. As in parenthetical references (see 5.3), the information included must be enough to identify the work. The author's last name alone, followed by the relevant page numbers, is usually adequate.

4 Frye 345-47.

If two or more works by the same author are cited—for example, Northrop Frye's *Anatomy of Criticism* as well as his *Critical Path*—a shortened form of the title should follow the author's last name in references after the first.

8 Frye, <u>Anatomy</u> 278.

9 Frye, <u>Critical</u> 1-10.

The information is repeated even when two references in sequence refer to the same work. The abbreviations "ibid." and "op. cit." are no longer used.

## 5.9.   Other style manuals

Every scholarly field has its preferred format or "style." MLA style, as presented in this manual, is widely accepted in humanities disciplines. The following manuals describe the styles of other disciplines:

### Biology

Council of Biology Editors. Style Manual Committee. *CBE Style Manual: A Guide for Authors, Editors, and Publishers in the Biological Sciences.* 5th ed. Bethesda: Council of Biology Editors, 1983.

### Chemistry

American Chemical Society. *Handbook for Authors of Papers in American Chemical Society Publications.* Washington: American Chemical Soc., 1978.

### Geology

United States. Geological Survey. *Suggestions to Authors of the Reports of the United States Geological Survey.* 6th ed. Washington: GPO, 1978.

### Linguistics

Linguistic Society of America. *LSA Bulletin,* Dec. issue, annually.

### Mathematics

American Mathematical Society. *A Manual for Authors of Mathematical Papers.* 7th ed. Providence: American Mathematical Soc., 1980.

### Medicine

International Steering Committee of Medical Editors. "Uniform Requirements for Manuscripts Submitted to Biomedical Journals." *Annals of Internal Medicine* 90 (Jan. 1979): 95–99.

### Physics

American Institute of Physics. Publications Board. *Style Manual for Guidance in the Preparation of Papers.* 3rd ed. New York: American Inst. of Physics, 1978.

### Psychology

American Psychological Association. *Publication Manual of the American Psychological Association.* 3rd ed. Washington: American Psychological Assn., 1983.

Other available style manuals are addressed primarily to editors and concern procedures for converting a manuscript into type:

*Chicago Manual of Style.* 13th ed. Chicago: U of Chicago P, 1982.

United States. Government Printing Office. *Style Manual*. Rev. ed.
    Washington: GPO, 1973.
*Words into Type*. By Marjorie E. Skillin, Robert M. Gay, et al. 3rd ed.
    Englewood Cliffs: Prentice, 1974.

For other style manuals and authors' guides, see John Bruce Howell,
*Style Manuals of the English-Speaking World* (Phoenix: Oryx, 1983).

# 6 ABBREVIATIONS AND REFERENCE WORDS

## 6.1. Introduction

Abbreviations are commonly used in the list of works cited and in tabular material but rarely in the text of a research paper (except within parentheses). In choosing abbreviations, keep your audience in mind. While economy of space is important, clarity is more so. Spell out a term if the abbreviation may puzzle your readers.

When abbreviating, always use commonly accepted forms. In appropriate contexts, you may abbreviate days, months, and other measurements of time (see 6.2); states and countries (see 6.3); terms and reference words common in scholarship (see 6.4); and publishers' names (see 6.5).

The trend in abbreviation is to use neither periods after letters nor spaces between letters, especially for abbreviations made up of all capital letters.

BC     NJ     PhD     S

The chief exception to this trend continues to be the initials used for personal names: a period and a space ordinarily follow each initial.

H. L. Mencken

Likewise, most abbreviations that end in lowercase letters are followed by periods.

assn.   Eng.   fig.   introd.   Mex.   prod.

Whenever such an abbreviation is part of a longer one, the other parts also take periods and spaces.

H. Doc.     n. pag.     U. S. Dept. of Labor

In most abbreviations made up of single lowercase letters, a period follows each letter, with no spaces between letters.

a.m.     e.g.     i.e.     n.p.

But there are numerous exceptions.

ips     ns     os     rpm

## 6.2.  Time

Spell out the names of months in the text but abbreviate them in the list of works cited, except for May, June, and July. Whereas words denoting units of time are also spelled out in the text (seconds, minutes, weeks, months, years, centuries), some time designations are used *only* in abbreviated form (a.m., p.m., AD, BC, BCE, CE).

| | |
|---|---|
| AD | *anno Domini* 'in the year of the Lord' (used before numerals: AD 14) |
| a.m. | *ante meridiem* 'before noon' |
| Apr. | April |
| Aug. | August |
| BC | before Christ (used after numerals: 19 BC) |
| BCE | before the Common Era |
| CE | Common Era |
| cent., cents. | century, centuries |
| Dec. | December |
| Feb. | February |
| Fri. | Friday |
| hr., hrs. | hour, hours |
| Jan. | January |
| Mar. | March |
| min., mins. | minute, minutes |
| mo., mos. | month, months |
| Mon. | Monday |
| Nov. | November |
| Oct. | October |
| p.m. | *post meridiem* 'after noon' |
| Sat. | Saturday |
| sec., secs. | second, seconds |
| Sept. | September |
| Sun. | Sunday |
| Thurs. | Thursday |
| Tues. | Tuesday |
| Wed. | Wednesday |
| wk., wks. | week, weeks |
| yr., yrs. | year, years |

## 6.3.  Geographical names

Spell out the names of states, territories, and possessions of the United States in the text, except, usually, in addresses and sometimes in pa-

rentheses. Likewise, spell out in the text the names of countries, with a
few exceptions (e.g., USSR, BRD, DDR). In documentation, however,
abbreviate the names of states, provinces, and countries.

| | |
|---|---|
| Afr. | Africa |
| AK | Alaska |
| AL | Alabama |
| Alb. | Albania |
| AR | Arkansas |
| Arg. | Argentina |
| Arm. | Armenia |
| AS | American Samoa |
| Aus. | Austria |
| Austral. | Australia |
| AZ | Arizona |
| Belg. | Belgium |
| Braz. | Brazil |
| BRD | Bundesrepublik Deutschland (see also W. Ger.) |
| Bulg. | Bulgaria |
| CA | California |
| Can. | Canada |
| CO | Colorado |
| CT | Connecticut |
| CZ | Canal Zone |
| Czech. | Czechoslovakia |
| DC | District of Columbia |
| DDR | Deutsche Demokratische Republik (see also E. Ger.) |
| DE | Delaware |
| Den. | Denmark |
| Ecua. | Ecuador |
| E. Ger. | East Germany (see also DDR) |
| Eng. | England |
| FL | Florida |
| Fr. | France |
| GA | Georgia |
| Gr. | Greece |
| Gt. Brit. | Great Britain |
| GU | Guam |
| HI | Hawaii |
| Hung. | Hungary |
| IA | Iowa |

| | |
|---|---|
| ID | Idaho |
| IL | Illinois |
| IN | Indiana |
| Ire. | Ireland |
| Isr. | Israel |
| It. | Italy |
| Jap. | Japan |
| KS | Kansas |
| KY | Kentucky |
| LA | Louisiana |
| Leb. | Lebanon |
| MA | Massachusetts |
| MD | Maryland |
| ME | Maine |
| Mex. | Mexico |
| MI | Michigan |
| MN | Minnesota |
| MO | Missouri |
| MS | Mississippi |
| MT | Montana |
| NC | North Carolina |
| ND | North Dakota |
| NE | Nebraska |
| Neth. | Netherlands |
| NH | New Hampshire |
| NJ | New Jersey |
| NM | New Mexico |
| Norw. | Norway |
| NV | Nevada |
| NY | New York |
| NZ | New Zealand |
| OH | Ohio |
| OK | Oklahoma |
| OR | Oregon |
| PA | Pennsylvania |
| Pan. | Panama |
| Pol. | Poland |
| Port. | Portugal |
| PR | Puerto Rico |
| PRC | People's Republic of China |
| RI | Rhode Island |
| SC | South Carolina |
| Scot. | Scotland |

| | |
|---|---|
| SD | South Dakota |
| S. Afr. | South Africa |
| Sp. | Spain |
| Swed. | Sweden |
| Switz. | Switzerland |
| TN | Tennessee |
| TX | Texas |
| Turk. | Turkey |
| UK | United Kingdom |
| US, USA | United States, United States of America |
| USSR | Union of Soviet Socialist Republics |
| UT | Utah |
| VA | Virginia |
| VI | Virgin Islands |
| VT | Vermont |
| WA | Washington |
| W. Ger. | West Germany (see also BRD) |
| WI | Wisconsin |
| WV | West Virginia |
| WY | Wyoming |
| Yug. | Yugoslavia |

## 6.4.  Common scholarly abbreviations and reference words

The following list includes both abbreviations and reference words commonly used in humanities research studies in English. Abbreviations within parentheses are alternative, but not preferred, forms. Most of the abbreviations listed would replace the spelled forms only in parentheses, tabular material, or documentation.

| | |
|---|---|
| abbr. | abbreviation, abbreviated |
| abr. | abridged, abridgment |
| acad. | academy |
| adapt. | adapted by, adaptation |
| adj. | adjective |
| adv. | adverb |
| anon. | anonymous |
| app. | appendix |
| arch. | archaic |
| art. | article |
| assn. | association |

| | |
|---|---|
| assoc. | associate, associated |
| attrib. | attributed to |
| aux. | auxiliary |
| b. | born |
| BA | Bachelor of Arts |
| bib. | biblical |
| bibliog. | bibliography, bibliographer, bibliographical |
| biog. | biography, biographer, biographical |
| bk. | book |
| BM | British Museum, London (now British Library) |
| BS | Bachelor of Science |
| bull. | bulletin |
| © | copyright (© 1984) |
| c. (ca.) | *circa* 'about' (used with approximate dates: c. 1796) |
| cf. | *confer* 'compare' (*not* 'see') |
| ch. (chap.) | chapter |
| chor. | choreographed by, choreographer |
| col. | column |
| coll. | college |
| colloq. | colloquial |
| comp. | compiled by, compiler |
| cond. | conducted by, conductor |
| Cong. | Congress |
| *Cong. Rec.* | *Congressional Record* |
| conj. | conjunction |
| Const. | Constitution |
| cont. | contents; continued |
| (contd.) | continued |
| d. | died |
| DA | Doctor of Arts |
| *DA, DAI* | *Dissertation Abstracts, Dissertation Abstracts International* |
| *DAB* | *Dictionary of American Biography* |
| dept. | department |
| dev. | developed by, development |
| dir. | directed by, director |
| diss. | dissertation |
| dist. | district |
| distr. | distributed by, distributor |
| div. | division |
| *DNB* | *Dictionary of National Biography* |

| | |
|---|---|
| doc. | document |
| ed. | edited by, editor, edition |
| EdD | Doctor of Education |
| educ. | education, educational |
| e.g. | *exempli gratia* 'for example' (rarely capitalized; set off by commas, unless preceded by a different punctuation mark) |
| enl. | enlarged (as in "rev. and enl. ed.") |
| esp. | especially |
| et al. | *et alii* 'and others' |
| etc. | *et cetera* 'and so forth' (like most abbreviations, not appropriate in text) |
| ex. | example |
| fac. | faculty |
| fig. | figure |
| fl. | *floruit* 'flourished, reached greatest development or influence' (used before dates of historical figures when birth and death dates are not known) |
| fr. | from; frame, frames |
| front. | frontispiece |
| fut. | future |
| fwd. | foreword, foreword by |
| gen. | general (as in "gen. ed.") |
| govt. | government |
| GPO | Government Printing Office, Washington, DC |
| H. Doc. | House Document |
| hist. | history, historian, historical |
| HMSO | Her (His) Majesty's Stationery Office |
| HR | House of Representatives |
| H. Rept. | House [of Representatives] Report |
| H. Res. | House [of Representatives] Resolution |
| i.e. | *id est* 'that is' (rarely capitalized; set off by commas, unless preceded by a different punctuation mark) |
| illus. | illustrated by, illustrator, illustration |
| inc. | incorporated; including |
| infin. | infinitive |
| inst. | institute, institution |
| intl. | international |
| introd. | (author of) introduction, introduced by, introduction |
| ips | inches per second (used in reference to recording tapes) |

| | |
|---|---|
| irreg. | irregular |
| jour. | journal |
| Jr. | Junior |
| KB | kilobytes |
| l., ll. | line, lines (avoided in favor of "line" and "lines" or, if clear, numbers only) |
| lang. | language |
| LC | Library of Congress |
| leg. | legal |
| legis. | legislation, legislative, legislature, legislator |
| lit. | literally; literary, literature |
| LLB | *Legum Baccalaureus* 'Bachelor of Laws' |
| LLD | *Legum Doctor* 'Doctor of Laws' |
| ltd. | limited |
| MA | Master of Arts |
| mag. | magazine |
| MD | *Medicinae Doctor* 'Doctor of Medicine' |
| misc. | miscellaneous |
| ms., mss. | manuscript, manuscripts (the many mss. of Chaucer; Bodleian ms. Tanner 43) |
| MS | Master of Science |
| n, nn | note, notes (used immediately after page number: 56n, 56n3, 56nn3–5) |
| n. | noun |
| narr. | narrated by, narrator |
| natl. | national |
| NB | *nota bene* 'take notice, mark well' (always capitalized) |
| n.d. | no date (of publication) |
| *NED* | *New English Dictionary* (cf. *OED*) |
| no. | number (cf. "numb.") |
| nonstand. | nonstandard |
| n.p. | no place (of publication); no publisher |
| n. pag. | no pagination |
| ns | new series |
| NS | New Style (calendar) |
| numb. | numbered |
| obj. | object, objective |
| obs. | obsolete |
| *OED* | *Oxford English Dictionary* (formerly *New English Dictionary* [*NED*]) |
| op. | opus (work) |
| orch. | orchestra, orchestrated by |

| | |
|---|---|
| orig. | original, originally |
| os | old series; original series |
| OS | Old Style (calendar) |
| p., pp. | page, pages (omitted before page numbers unless reference otherwise would be unclear) |
| P | Press (used in documentation; see "UP") |
| par. | paragraph |
| part. | participle |
| perf. | performer, performed by |
| PhD | *Philosophiae Doctor* 'Doctor of Philosophy' |
| philol. | philological |
| philos. | philosophical |
| pl. | plate; plural |
| poss. | possessive |
| pref. | preface, preface by |
| prep. | preposition |
| pres. | present |
| proc. | proceedings |
| prod. | produced by, producer |
| pron. | pronoun |
| pronunc. | pronunciation |
| PS | postscript |
| pseud. | pseudonym |
| pt. | part |
| pub (publ.) | published by, publisher, publication |
| r. | reigned |
| rec. | recorded, record |
| reg. | registered; regular |
| rept. | reported by, report |
| res. | resolution |
| resp. | respectively |
| rev. | revised by, revision; review, reviewed by (spell out "review" where "rev." might be ambiguous) |
| rpm | revolutions per minute (used in reference to recordings) |
| rpt. | reprinted by, reprint |
| S | Senate |
| sc. | scene (omitted when act and scene numbers are used together: *Lear* 4.1) |
| S. Doc. | Senate Document |
| sec. (sect.) | section |
| ser. | series |
| sess. | session |

| | |
|---|---|
| sic | "thus, so" (placed within square brackets when used as an editorial interpolation [see 2.6.5], otherwise in parentheses; not followed by an exclamation mark) |
| sing. | singular |
| soc. | society |
| Sr. | Senior |
| S. Rept. | Senate Report |
| S. Res. | Senate Resolution |
| st. | stanza |
| St., Sts. (S, SS) | Saint, Saints |
| subj. | subject, subjective; subjunctive |
| substand. | substandard |
| supp. | supplement |
| syn. | synonym |
| trans. (tr.) | translated by, translator, translation; transitive |
| ts., tss. | typescript, typescripts (cf. "ms.") |
| U | University (used in documentation; see "UP") |
| UP | University Press (used in documentation: Columbia UP) |
| usu. | usually |
| v., vv. (vs., vss.) | verse, verses (cf. "vs. (v.)") |
| var. | variant |
| vb. | verb |
| vol., vols. | volume, volumes |
| vs. (v.) | versus 'against' (v. preferred in titles of legal cases; cf. "v., vv.") |
| writ. | written by, writer |

# 6.5.  Publishers' names

## 6.5.1.  General guidelines

Shortened forms of publishers' names are included in the list of works cited, immediately after the city of publication, to enable the reader to locate a book or to acquire more information about it. Since publishers' addresses are listed in such books as *Books in Print, Literary Market Place,* and *International Literary Market Place,* you need give only enough information so that your reader can look up the publisher in one of these sources. It is usually sufficient, for example, to give as the publisher's name "Harcourt" even if the title page indicates "Harcourt Brace Jovanovich" or one of the earlier names of that firm (Harcourt;

Harcourt, Brace; Harcourt, Brace, and World). If you are preparing a bibliographical study, however, or if publication history is important to your paper, give the publisher's name in full. In shortening publishers' names, keep in mind the following:

1.  Omit articles, business abbreviations (e.g., Co., Corp., Inc., Ltd.), and descriptive words (e.g., Books, House, Press, Publishers). When citing a university press, however, always add the abbreviation "P" (e.g., Ohio State UP) because the university itself may publish independently of its press (e.g., Ohio State U).

2.  If the publisher's name includes the name of one person, cite the last name alone (e.g., Abrams, Heath, Norton, Wiley). If the publisher's name includes the names of more than one person, cite only the first of these names (e.g., Bobbs, Dodd, Faber, Farrar, Funk, Grosset, Harcourt, Harper, Holt, Houghton, McGraw, Prentice, Simon).

3.  Use standard abbreviations whenever possible (e.g., Acad., Assn., Soc., UP).

4.  If the publisher's name is commonly abbreviated with capital initial letters and if the abbreviation is likely to be familiar to your audience, use the abbreviation as the publisher's name (e.g., GPO, MLA, UMI). If your readers are not likely to know the abbreviation, shorten the name according to the general guidelines given above (e.g., Mod. Lang. Assn., etc.).

## 6.5.2.  Selected publishers' names

Acceptable shortened forms of publishers' names include the following:

| | |
|---|---|
| Abrams | Harry N. Abrams, Inc. |
| Acad. for Educ. Dev. | Academy for Educational Development, Inc. |
| Allen | George Allen and Unwin Publishers, Inc. |
| Allyn | Allyn and Bacon, Inc. |
| Appleton | Appleton-Century-Crofts |
| Ballantine | Ballantine Books, Inc. |
| Bantam | Bantam Books, Inc. |
| Barnes | Barnes and Noble Books |
| Basic | Basic Books |
| Beacon | Beacon Press, Inc. |
| Benn | Ernest Benn, Ltd. |
| Bobbs | The Bobbs-Merrill Co., Inc. |
| Bowker | R. R. Bowker Co. |
| CAL | Center for Applied Linguistics |

| | |
|---|---|
| Cambridge UP | Cambridge University Press |
| Clarendon | Clarendon Press |
| Columbia UP | Columbia University Press |
| Cornell UP | Cornell University Press |
| Dell | Dell Publishing Co., Inc. |
| Dodd | Dodd, Mead, and Co. |
| Doubleday | Doubleday and Co., Inc. |
| Dover | Dover Publications, Inc. |
| Dutton | E. P. Dutton, Inc. |
| Farrar | Farrar, Straus, and Giroux, Inc. |
| Feminist | The Feminist Press |
| Free | The Free Press |
| Funk | Funk and Wagnalls, Inc. |
| Gale | Gale Research Co. |
| GPO | Government Printing Office |
| Harcourt | Harcourt Brace Jovanovich, Inc. |
| Harper | Harper and Row Publishers, Inc. |
| Harvard Law Rev. Assn. | Harvard Law Review Association |
| Harvard UP | Harvard University Press |
| Heath | D. C. Heath and Co. |
| HMSO | Her (His) Majesty's Stationery Office |
| Holt | Holt, Rinehart, and Winston, Inc. |
| Houghton | Houghton Mifflin Co. |
| Humanities | Humanities Press, Inc. |
| Indiana UP | Indiana University Press |
| Johns Hopkins UP | The Johns Hopkins University Press |
| Knopf | Alfred A. Knopf, Inc. |
| Larousse | Librairie Larousse |
| Lippincott | J. B. Lippincott Co. |
| Little | Little, Brown, and Co. |
| Macmillan | Macmillan Publishing Co., Inc. |
| McGraw | McGraw-Hill, Inc. |
| MIT P | The MIT Press |
| MLA | The Modern Language Association of America |
| NAL | The New American Library, Inc. |
| NCTE | The National Council of Teachers of English |
| NEA | The National Education Association |
| New York Graphic Soc. | New York Graphic Society |
| Norton | W. W. Norton and Co., Inc. |
| Oxford UP | Oxford University Press, Inc. |

| | |
|---|---|
| ₋nguin | Penguin Books, Inc. |
| Pocket | Pocket Books |
| Popular | The Popular Press |
| Prentice | Prentice-Hall, Inc. |
| Princeton UP | Princeton University Press |
| Putnam's | G. P. Putnam's Sons |
| Rand | Rand McNally and Co. |
| Random | Random House, Inc. |
| Rizzoli | Rizzoli Editore |
| St. Martin's | St. Martin's Press, Inc. |
| Scott | Scott, Foresman, and Co. |
| Scribner's | Charles Scribner's Sons |
| Simon | Simon and Schuster, Inc. |
| State U of New York P | State University of New York Press |
| UMI | University Microfilms International |
| U of Chicago P | University of Chicago Press |
| U of Toronto P | University of Toronto Press |
| UP of Florida | The University Presses of Florida |
| Viking | The Viking Press, Inc. |
| Yale UP | Yale University Press |

## 6.6. Symbols and abbreviations used in proofreading and correction

### 6.6.1. Selected proofreading symbols

The symbols below are used in proofreading typeset material. Many instructors use them in correcting student papers.

| | |
|---|---|
| ⱱ | Apostrophe or single quotation mark |
| ⊂ | Close up (baske⌒ball) |
| ⋏ | Comma |
| ⋊ | Delete |
| ⋏ | Insert |
| ¶ | Begin a new paragraph |
| No ¶ | Do not begin a new paragraph |
| ⊙ | Period |
| ⱽ ⱽ | Double quotation marks |
| # | Space |
| ∿ | Transpose elements, usually with "tr" in margin (th⌢er) |

## 6.6.2. Common correction symbols and abbreviations

| Ab | Faulty abbreviation |
|----|---------------------|
| Adj | Improper use of adjective |
| Adv | Improper use of adverb |
| Agr | Faulty agreement |
| Amb | Ambiguous |
| Awk | Awkward expression or construction |
| Cap | Faulty capitalization |
| D | Faulty diction |
| Dgl | Dangling construction |
| Frag | Fragment |
| lc | Use lowercase |
| Num | Error in use of numbers |
| ‖ | Lack of parallelism |
| P | Faulty punctuation |
| Ref | Unclear pronoun reference |
| Rep | Unnecessary repetition |
| R-O | Run-on |
| Sp | Error in spelling |
| SS | Faulty sentence structure |
| T | Wrong tense of verb |
| tr | Transpose elements |
| V | Wrong verb form |
| Wdy | Wordy |

*[handwritten margin notes:]*
*CL – Clarity*
*COH – Coherence*
*W.O Word order*
*K – awkward*
*Lev – level of usage*

*Universals –*
*(universal statement – Can be no exceptions)*
*qualify w/ most*
*Its no-no list*
*None – verb singular*
*neither – a or b is*
*unique – or not can't be*
*(almost unique or somewhat unique*
*its – it's*

# 6.7. Literary and religious works

The following are examples of abbreviations that may be used in documentation; it is usually best to introduce the abbreviation in parentheses immediately after the first use of the full title in the text: "In *Paradise Lost (PL)*, Milton. . . ." For works not on these lists, you may use the abbreviations you find in your research or devise simple, unambiguous abbreviations of your own.

## 6.7.1. Bible (Bib.)

The following abbreviations and spelled forms are commonly used for parts of the Bible.

### Old Testament (OT)

| Gen. | Genesis |
|------|---------|
| Exod. | Exodus |
| Lev. | Leviticus |

| | |
|---|---|
| Num. | Numbers |
| Deut. | Deuteronomy |
| Josh. | Joshua |
| Judg. | Judges |
| Ruth | Ruth |
| 1 Sam. | 1 Samuel |
| 2 Sam. | 2 Samuel |
| 1 Kings | 1 Kings |
| 2 Kings | 2 Kings |
| 1 Chron. | 1 Chronicles |
| 2 Chron. | 2 Chronicles |
| Ezra | Ezra |
| Neh. | Nehemiah |
| Esth. | Esther |
| Job | Job |
| Ps. | Psalms |
| Prov. | Proverbs |
| Eccles. | Ecclesiastes |
| Song Sol. (also Cant.) | Song of Solomon (also Canticles) |
| Isa. | Isaiah |
| Jer. | Jeremiah |
| Lam. | Lamentations |
| Ezek. | Ezekiel |
| Dan. | Daniel |
| Hos. | Hosea |
| Joel | Joel |
| Amos | Amos |
| Obad. | Obadiah |
| Jon. | Jonah |
| Mic. | Micah |
| Nah. | Nahum |
| Hab. | Habakkuk |
| Zeph. | Zephaniah |
| Hag. | Haggai |
| Zech. | Zechariah |
| Mal. | Malachi |

### *Selected Apocryphal and Deuterocanonical Works*

| | |
|---|---|
| 1 Esd. | 1 Esdras |
| 2 Esd. | 2 Esdras |
| Tob. | Tobit |
| Jth. | Judith |

| | |
|---|---|
| Esth. (Apocr.) | Esther (Apocrypha) |
| Wisd. Sol. (also Wisd.) | Wisdom of Solomon (also Wisdom) |
| Ecclus. (also Sir.) | Ecclesiasticus (also Sirach) |
| Bar. | Baruch |
| Song 3 Childr. | Song of the Three Children |
| Sus. | Susanna |
| Bel and Dr. | Bel and the Dragon |
| Pr. Man. | Prayer of Manasseh |
| 1 Macc. | 1 Maccabees |
| 2 Macc. | 2 Maccabees |

**New Testament (NT)**

| | |
|---|---|
| Matt. | Matthew |
| Mark | Mark |
| Luke | Luke |
| John | John |
| Acts | Acts |
| Rom. | Romans |
| 1 Cor. | 1 Corinthians |
| 2 Cor. | 2 Corinthians |
| Gal. | Galatians |
| Eph. | Ephesians |
| Phil. | Philippians |
| Col. | Colossians |
| 1 Thess. | 1 Thessalonians |
| 2 Thess. | 2 Thessalonians |
| 1 Tim. | 1 Timothy |
| 2 Tim. | 2 Timothy |
| Tit. | Titus |
| Philem. | Philemon |
| Heb. | Hebrews |
| Jas. | James |
| 1 Pet. | 1 Peter |
| 2 Pet. | 2 Peter |
| 1 John | 1 John |
| 2 John | 2 John |
| 3 John | 3 John |
| Jude | Jude |
| Rev. (also Apoc.) | Revelation (also Apocalypse) |

### Selected Apocryphal Works

| | |
|---|---|
| G. Thom. | Gospel of Thomas |
| G. Heb. | Gospel of the Hebrews |
| G. Pet. | Gospel of Peter |

## 6.7.2.  Shakespeare

| | |
|---|---|
| *Ado* | *Much Ado about Nothing* |
| *Ant.* | *Antony and Cleopatra* |
| *AWW* | *All's Well That Ends Well* |
| *AYL* | *As You Like It* |
| *Cor.* | *Coriolanus* |
| *Cym.* | *Cymbeline* |
| *Err.* | *The Comedy of Errors* |
| *F1* | First Folio ed. (1623) |
| *F2* | Second Folio ed. (1632) |
| *Ham.* | *Hamlet* |
| *1H4* | *Henry IV, Part 1* |
| *2H4* | *Henry IV, Part 2* |
| *H5* | *Henry V* |
| *1H6* | *Henry VI, Part 1* |
| *2H6* | *Henry VI, Part 2* |
| *3H6* | *Henry VI, Part 3* |
| *H8* | *Henry VIII* |
| *JC* | *Julius Caesar* |
| *Jn.* | *King John* |
| *LC* | *A Lover's Complaint* |
| *LLL* | *Love's Labour's Lost* |
| *Lr.* | *King Lear* |
| *Luc.* | *The Rape of Lucrece* |
| *Mac.* | *Macbeth* |
| *MM* | *Measure for Measure* |
| *MND* | *A Midsummer Night's Dream* |
| *MV* | *The Merchant of Venice* |
| *Oth.* | *Othello* |
| *Per.* | *Pericles* |
| *PhT* | *The Phoenix and the Turtle* |
| *PP* | *The Passionate Pilgrim* |
| *Q* | Quarto ed. |
| *R2* | *Richard II* |
| *R3* | *Richard III* |
| *Rom.* | *Romeo and Juliet* |
| *Shr.* | *The Taming of the Shrew* |

| | |
|---|---|
| *Son.* | *Sonnets* |
| *TGV* | *The Two Gentlemen of Verona* |
| *Tim.* | *Timon of Athens* |
| *Tit.* | *Titus Andronicus* |
| *Tmp.* | *The Tempest* |
| *TN* | *Twelfth Night* |
| *TNK* | *The Two Noble Kinsmen* |
| *Tro.* | *Troilus and Cressida* |
| *Ven.* | *Venus and Adonis* |
| *Wiv.* | *The Merry Wives of Windsor* |
| *WT* | *The Winter's Tale* |

## 6.7.3.  Chaucer

| | |
|---|---|
| CkT | The Cook's Tale |
| ClT | The Clerk's Tale |
| *CT* | *The Canterbury Tales* |
| CYT | The Canon's Yeoman's Tale |
| FranT | The Franklin's Tale |
| FrT | The Friar's Tale |
| GP | The General Prologue |
| KnT | The Knight's Tale |
| ManT | The Manciple's Tale |
| Mel | The Tale of Melibee |
| MerT | The Merchant's Tale |
| MilT | The Miller's Tale |
| MkT | The Monk's Tale |
| MLT | The Man of Law's Tale |
| NPT | The Nun's Priest's Tale |
| PardT | The Pardoner's Tale |
| ParsT | The Parson's Tale |
| PhyT | The Physician's Tale |
| PrT | The Prioress's Tale |
| Ret | Chaucer's Retraction |
| RvT | The Reeve's Tale |
| ShT | The Shipman's Tale |
| SNT | The Second Nun's Tale |
| SqT | The Squire's Tale |
| SumT | The Summoner's Tale |
| Th | The Tale of Sir Thopas |
| WBT | The Wife of Bath's Tale |

## 6.7.4.  Other literary works

| | |
|---|---|
| *Aen.* | Vergil, *Aeneid* |
| *Ag.* | Aeschylus, *Agamemnon* |
| *Ant.* | Sophocles, *Antigone* |
| *Bac.* | Euripides, *Bacchae* |
| *Beo.* | *Beowulf* |
| *Can.* | Voltaire, *Candide* |
| *Dec.* | Boccaccio, *Decamerone* |
| *DJ* | Byron, *Don Juan* |
| *DQ* | Cervantes, *Don Quixote* |
| *Eum.* | Aeschylus, *Eumenides* |
| *FQ* | Spenser, *Faerie Queene* |
| *Gil.* | *Epic of Gilgamesh* |
| *GT* | Swift, *Gulliver's Travels* |
| *Hept.* | Marguerite de Navarre, *Heptaméron* |
| *Hip.* | Euripides, *Hippolytus* |
| *Il.* | Homer, *Iliad* |
| *Inf.* | Dante, *Inferno* |
| *LB* | Wordsworth, *Lyrical Ballads* |
| *Lys.* | Aristophanes, *Lysistrata* |
| *Med.* | Euripides, *Medea* |
| *MD* | Melville, *Moby-Dick* |
| *Mis.* | Molière, *Misanthrope* |
| *Nib.* | *Nibelungenlied* |
| *Od.* | Homer, *Odyssey* |
| *OF* | Ariosto, *Orlando Furioso* |
| *Or.* | Aeschylus, *Oresteia* |
| *OR* | Sophocles, *Oedipus Rex* (also called *Oedipus Tyrannus* [*OT*]) |
| *OT* | Sophocles, *Oedipus Tyrannus* (also called *Oedipus Rex* [*OR*]) |
| *Par.* | Dante, *Paradiso* |
| *PL* | Milton, *Paradise Lost* |
| *Prel.* | Wordsworth, *Prelude* |
| *Purg.* | Dante, *Purgatorio* |
| *Rep.* | Plato, *Republic* |
| *SA* | Milton, *Samson Agonistes* |
| *SGGK* | *Sir Gawain and the Green Knight* |
| *Sym.* | Plato, *Symposium* |
| *Tar.* | Molière, *Tartuffe* |

# SAMPLE PAGES OF A RESEARCH PAPER

# First page of a research paper

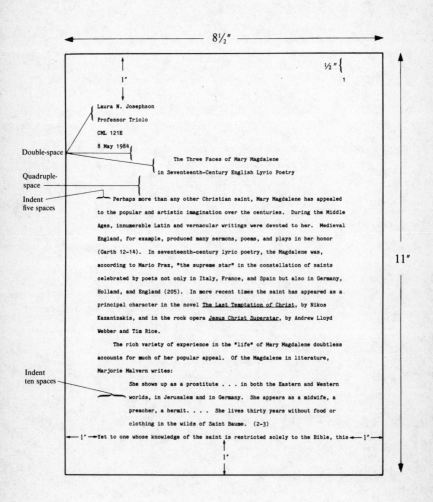

8½"

½" {
1

1"

Laura N. Josephson

Professor Triolo

CML 121E

**Double-space** ← 8 May 1984

The Three Faces of Mary Magdalene

in Seventeenth-Century English Lyric Poetry

**Quadruple-space** ←

**Indent five spaces** → Perhaps more than any other Christian saint, Mary Magdalene has appealed

to the popular and artistic imagination over the centuries. During the Middle

Ages, innumerable Latin and vernacular writings were devoted to her. Medieval

England, for example, produced many sermons, poems, and plays in her honor

(Garth 12-14). In seventeenth-century lyric poetry, the Magdalene was,

according to Mario Praz, "the supreme star" in the constellation of saints

celebrated by poets not only in Italy, France, and Spain but also in Germany,

Holland, and England (205). In more recent times the saint has appeared as a

principal character in the novel The Last Temptation of Christ, by Nikos

Kazantzakis, and in the rock opera Jesus Christ Superstar, by Andrew Lloyd

Webber and Tim Rice.

The rich variety of experience in the "life" of Mary Magdalene doubtless

accounts for much of her popular appeal. Of the Magdalene in literature,

Marjorie Malvern writes:

**Indent ten spaces** → She shows up as a prostitute . . . in both the Eastern and Western

worlds, in Jerusalem and in Germany. She appears as a midwife, a

preacher, a hermit. . . . She lives thirty years without food or

clothing in the wilds of Saint Baume. (2-3)

← 1" → Yet to one whose knowledge of the saint is restricted solely to the Bible, this ← 1" →

1"

11"

# First page of Works Cited

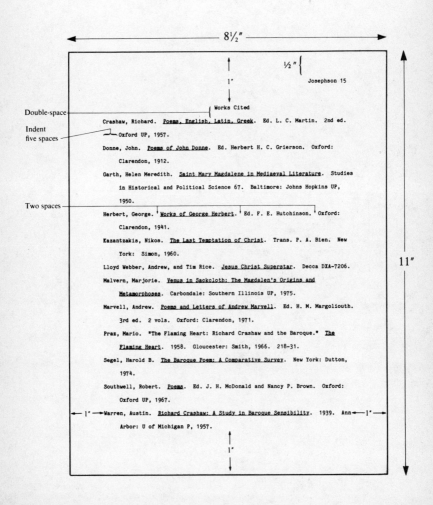

Double-space

Indent
five spaces

Two spaces

Josephson 15

Works Cited

Crashaw, Richard. _Poems, English, Latin, Greek_. Ed. L. C. Martin. 2nd ed.

Oxford UP, 1957.

Donne, John. _Poems of John Donne_. Ed. Herbert H. C. Grierson. Oxford:

Clarendon, 1912.

Garth, Helen Meredith. _Saint Mary Magdalene in Mediaeval Literature_. Studies

in Historical and Political Science 67. Baltimore: Johns Hopkins UP,

1950.

Herbert, George. _Works of George Herbert_. Ed. F. E. Hutchinson. Oxford:

Clarendon, 1941.

Kazantzakis, Nikos. _The Last Temptation of Christ_. Trans. P. A. Bien. New

York: Simon, 1960.

Lloyd Webber, Andrew, and Tim Rice. _Jesus Christ Superstar_. Decca DXA-7206.

Malvern, Marjorie. _Venus in Sackcloth: The Magdalen's Origins and

Metamorphoses_. Carbondale: Southern Illinois UP, 1975.

Marvell, Andrew. _Poems and Letters of Andrew Marvell_. Ed. H. M. Margoliouth.

3rd ed. 2 vols. Oxford: Clarendon, 1971.

Praz, Mario. "The Flaming Heart: Richard Crashaw and the Baroque." _The

Flaming Heart_. 1958. Gloucester: Smith, 1966. 218-31.

Segel, Harold B. _The Baroque Poem: A Comparative Survey_. New York: Dutton,

1974.

Southwell, Robert. _Poems_. Ed. J. H. McDonald and Nancy P. Brown. Oxford:

Oxford UP, 1967.

Warren, Austin. _Richard Crashaw: A Study in Baroque Sensibility_. 1939. Ann

Arbor: U of Michigan P, 1957.

# INDEX